BEYOND MY GREEN VALLEY

Other titles by the same author

Not Just a Berkshire Farmer
Just More of the Berkshire Farmer

Beyond my

GREEN VALLEY

by Bert Houghton

© A. F. (Bert) Houghton, Stable Cottage, Red Farm,
Long Lane, Shaw, Newbury, Berkshire RG14 2TE 1996
Telephone 01635 524331/40333

ISBN 0 9514193 2 3

Front cover photograph: My Green Valley

Produced through MRM Associates Ltd.,
Unit C4, Weldale Street, Reading, Berks RG1 7BX

CONTENTS

The Author

Foreword

My ever-widening circle of readers has once again urged me to write yet more of my stories. The problem is that I have run out of day to day farming incidents to relate and now that I am retired I have not kept up with the latest changes and technical advances in the farming world. I asked myself "Why not write about my travels and true adventures around the world?" Journeys to new and exciting places inhabited by people with different cultural backgrounds, out there

Beyond my Green Valley.

Fortunately I have always been an avid writer and over the years I have conscientiously kept up my diaries of events in my life so this has enabled me to write this book.

ACKNOWLEDGEMENTS
I would like to express my thanks to all those who have helped me with this book, but I am particularly indebted to the following people:-

My wife Ruth, to whom I have dedicated this book, for her constant encouragement and her assistance in jogging my flagging memory.

My step-daughter Mrs Sue Bourne for all her help and advice and for writing the introduction.

Mr David Brierly of Winterbourne and our wonderful neighbour Mrs Patricia Walker for all their work in editing.

My son-in law Mr Roger Bourne for the use of his computer and his editing skill.

And last but by no means least my two young assistants – my granddaughter Catherine Mant and her friend Nicola Krohn for all their patience in typing up my scrawly longhand.

My Green Valley

I believe that I have some claim to call it "my valley" since our four farms are situated within its boundaries and my family have farmed there for almost the whole of the twentieth century. From leaving school at the age of thirteen and a bit I never gave a thought to doing any job other than farming. Other lads at school wanted to drive fire engines, be policemen or work behind an office desk. I am fortunate that two of my five sons are as keen as I am on what I do. Returning from college with those all important pieces of paper – something I never obtained – they're always here to cultivate the fields, trim the hedges and tend our valued livestock 365 days a year. I won't be here for ever but I know it's all going to carry on through them. That gives me a feeling – not of immortality – but of peace, although at the end of the day we're here just as custodians, to look after it for future generations and those less fortunate than ourselves.

Officially described on maps as an area of outstanding natural beauty, the land lies between a range of two low hills bisected by the B4009 – a quiet country road, or at least it was until the arrival of the motor car! Mousefield Farm and Dymond Farm lie on the east side of this road with Red Farm and Grange Farm on the west marking the boundaries of the estate. This fertile land has been cultivated since mediaeval times and possibly since the Iron Age. There is some heavy clay but in the main the soil is sandy loam overlying chalk. Free draining the land can be worked almost any day of the year – a distinct advantage over the heavy clay soil in some parts of the country. A disadvantage, of course, is that it quickly dries out in a dry spell. During prolonged spells of rain water pours off the hillsides in ditches and streams seeking the lowest point. In the winter small lakes are often formed which last on the surface for only three or four days before the water vanishes through fissures in the underlying chalk. I'm sure there must be an underground river taking all the water away. In fact a neighbouring farming friend of mine tells me that his grandfather always insisted that from a secret spot one could move down through caverns in the chalk and walk this watercourse from Hermitage to Newbury, a distance of three miles. Another country gentleman, now unfortunately departed, swore that one day he had seen two ducks feeding in a small stream in full spate. Before his eyes they were swept away by the force of water only to vanish down a soak hole. Two days later he saw these same ducks swimming in the River Lambourn two miles away, proving indisputably that there is indeed an underground watercourse in this valley. I like to think that over the years my family have maintained this beautiful piece of countryside not just for ourselves but for all the folk who live nearby. Our land is criss-crossed by footpaths and a bridle-way and every Spring we open the woods to the public so that they too can enjoy, free of charge, these ancient coppiced woodlands through which we maintain nature trails for easy access. Beneath the canopy of giant oaks and silver birch trees the forest floor is a riot of colour. Bluebells, primroses, wood anemones and later the foxgloves and the honeysuckle. Wild life abounds, foxes, badgers and rabbits hide underground during the day venturing forth at dusk. Roe, fallow deer and the secretive muntjac seek the shelter of the glades. To rise early and listen to the dawn chorus in Spring is a tonic better than any medicine.

Luckily for those that appreciate the countryside, the market town of Newbury has not encroached northwards onto my land. Developers have desperately tried to purchase at various times but I have always resisted their offers. In fact I wrote to one persistent gentleman that I would rather see cows – my cows – grazing the meadows than to view a housing estate.

But as I grew older I didn't wish to spend the rest of my life tied to this small patch of Berkshire ignorant of what lay beyond my own boundary.

What was the rest of the world like? How did the other half live? What lay beyond my green valley? I resolved to find out and to experience first hand the wonders of the world.

I invite you the reader of this book to relax in a comfortable chair, a hammock in your garden or a sea-side deckchair and join me on my travels. You could even take it to bed to read but don't expect to get to sleep!

Canada

With an area of over 3,800,000 square miles, 40 times as large as Britain and 18 times as large as France, it is the second largest country in the world and in my opinion the second best.

With almost as many relatives in Canada as I have in England it is perhaps not surprising that I have come to recognise this vast land as my second home. My blood relatives in that part of the world are all descendants of my late Uncle Ralph and they are now scattered widely across the continent from East to West, a fact that has enabled me to enjoy some wonderful vacations and I've often been told, "Now don't you go bringing wads of that English money over here, we've got plenty of good Canadian dollars." I first visited Canada in 1972 in the company of my late wife. My younger sons were quite capable of running the family farm in my absence whilst at the same time older members of my family were away studying at university. My main objective on this trip was to seek out my Father's homestead.

Luckily I was in possession of the original deeds which gave the location of this speck of land as West of the 3rd Meridian in the Rural Municipality of Grass Lake Number 381 Reward, Saskatchewan and presently farmed by Chuck Deck and his family. My father, a real pioneer with a grim determination to succeed in any objective he set himself, had reached his goal in four months of travel, first by ship, then by the unreliable iron horse and the final six hundred miles on foot! At that time I didn't realise the sheer size of this vast land and the distances involved. Even with modern travel facilities, we failed to reach our objective in the time we had allowed ourselves.

I did make it some years later on my second attempt. Here I apologise that this fact is already mentioned in my previous book.

Peggy and I flew out of Heathrow on July 21st 1972 in a Jumbo 747. Destination Toronto. It was the first time my wife had flown and a first for me in a modern jet liner. Climbing quickly into the sunshine at 30,000 feet way above the cotton-wool clouds leaving rain drenched England far below, in no time at all we were enjoying complimentary drinks and salted peanuts over Scotland, lunch over the southern tip of Greenland-with its snow-capped mountains and giant icebergs floating offshore-to be followed by dinner over the frozen wastes of Northern Canada. After an eight hour flight and frequent time changes I had lost all track of time, what meal was what and whether I should be fully awake or fitfully sleeping, but such is the wonder of modern travel that in just a few hours one can be half way round the globe.

Peggy and I had diligently spent many a pleasant evening by the log fire at Mousefield planning our itinerary. With luck all should go smoothly, we would spend a few days sight-seeing in Toronto, pay a short visit to farming friends close by, then a few days in Ottawa before heading West by CN rail to Vancouver visiting friends and relatives en-route. From the travel agent in Newbury I ordered a hire car to await my collection at Toronto Airport, one which I could drive unlimited mileage and drop off anywhere in Canada when no longer required. "No, I don't want a small car, medium size, I told the agent. Canada hasn't got the car-parking problems which plague us in England, and I was fully aware that a large car rides better over unpaved roads. I also knew that some of my farming friends lived far off the beaten track.

Toronto International Airport:

Safely on terra firma we followed our fellow passengers like a flock of sheep rushing eagerly for the concentrates in the feed trough, only in our case it was to collect our luggage and be first through customs. There was no need to have rushed, it was thirty minutes before the first cases started their endless circuit on the moving rubber belt. "There's one of ours, grab it quick!" said Peggy, giving me a none-to gentle shove. Almost every passenger had left before I retrieved our fourth and last bulky piece of baggage. In the days and weeks that followed we were to regret dragging half our personal wardrobe thousands of miles across Canada. Most Canadians dress very informal, I never once wore my dinner suit nor did any occasion present itself for my wife to wear her best evening dress. In the arrival lounge were crowds of people of all nationalities with bodies pressed tight against the restraint barrier, some were holding up hastily written name cards eager to recognise visiting friends or relatives, some they may not have seen since childhood. We pushed our overloaded trolley through the melee of humanity. I stepped up to the service counter. "You have a car booked in the name of Houghton?" I asked the coloured attendant. He tapped his desk top, "Yep, that's correct". "Some paperwork for you to complete, insurance etc. then if you would kindly wait just outside the airport building through the main doors over there, I'll get someone to fetch your car over."

Moments later the hire car pulled noiselessly alongside, gleaming in the evening sunshine, metallic blue/grey with Ontario number plate our 'medium' size car was enormous. From the bumper to the boot -sorry, we were in Canada now- from the fender to the trunk it was 18 feet, more of a limousine suitable for the governor general. In fact it was the same length as my cattle wagon back home in which I could transport 60 fat hogs to the bacon factory or 10 half-ton barren cows to Banbury Market. Placing our luggage in the trunk I made to get into the car. "Steering wheel is on this side Sir." Sheepishly I said, " Why, yes of course it is."

Handing over the ignition key the attendant said, "I've filled her up with gas she is all yours, have a nice day." Then he was gone. Gingerly we climbed aboard where I soon discovered that the car was fully automatic, no clutch, just a foot brake and an accelerator. I'd never driven such a vehicle in my life, only the most expensive models had such refinements back in England.

Anxiously my wife said, " You can't drive this great thing, no gears to change, the steering wheel is on the wrong side and they drive on the right over here remember." " I'll darn well have a good try," I replied. "It's big enough, they will all have to get out of my way." I was forgetting that all the rest of the cars on the road were the same size or even larger.

Out of the airport complex onto 401, a six lane freeway, I joined the five o'clock rush hour. Ten miles on and still mobile, I managed to pull out of the traffic. Forking off to the right down Wesson Road which follows the Humber River valley until turning into Dundas Street W. making for our hotel in downtown Toronto. En route other road users had shown their displeasure with my driving. Some had waved their fists or blasted rudely on car horns, others had cut me up. What a journey but we made it in one piece. At the hotel entrance the commissionaire summoned an attendant to park my car, the bell boy took our luggage, I made for the bar. I sure needed a stiff drink!

We spent a week sightseeing in Toronto. The hotel was grand, the staff helpful and polite, the food first-rate. Our room sported a king size bed with an en-suite bathroom, and one could hang a small sign on the outside of the bedroom door

"Do not disturb". The farm with all it's daily problems and seven children were 3,000 odd miles away. It was indeed a second honeymoon and to cap it all we had our 'Limo' now proudly flying a Union Jack both fore and aft which certainly helped to keep irate drivers at a distance. When we did drive out of the city we even got salutes from the traffic control police!

Toronto with a population of 3 million is Canada's largest City. We decided to leave the car at the hotel car park preferring to walk or take public transport to view the sights. I wasn't over keen to drive the crowded streets and struggle to find a car parking space. Top priority for us was to visit the recently opened CN Tower which at that time claimed to be the world's tallest free standing structure. Glass sided elevators whisk one up to a revolving restaurant and observation deck from where one can view the whole city and look down on even the tallest skyscrapers. More down to earth attractions include the new Sky Dome, home of the Blue Jays, the City Hall with its curved twin towers encircling a three storey "Flying Saucer" and the coloured water fountains which are just brilliant at night. Dundas Street is the centre of Chinatown which I was told is larger than the celebrated equivalent in San Francisco. A great place to eat if you like Chinese cuisine. We are not great shoppers but for those folk with the inclination the Eaton Centre, a soaring glass and concrete complex that stretches four city blocks and houses over 300 individual shops, is just unbelievable. The Harbour Front, Ontario Place, Toronto Zoo with over 5,000 animals, the list is endless. We packed in a very full week.

One should not visit this part of the world without a trip to Niagara Falls, a sight which attracts tourists from around the globe. It also attracts honeymooners by the thousand, although nobody knows why. Legend has it that Napoleon's brother came by stage coach from New Orleans for his honeymoon and so set the trend. Why should Peggy and I be any different. We would go to the Falls.

Although not strictly correct we referred to our hire car as the limo, it sounded grand and it was fab. With great caution I slowly manoeuvred through early morning traffic out onto the Queen Elizabeth Freeway. With every mile I gain confidence. Slipping into cruise control at 100k -62 miles an hour-I only had to steer a straight course, miss all the other motorists and not fall asleep! Mississauga, Oakville, Burlington sped by then over the bridge in the sky at Hamilton which crosses the far western corner of Lake Ontario. In less than two hours we were at Niagara on the Lake.

Everything was so green and colourful, the manicured lawns, the magnificent rose gardens, the arboretum all kept to perfection by an army of dedicated gardeners and the continuous spray rising from the Falls. We sure crammed a lot into our one day visit. For a while Peggy and I just stood by the iron safety railings within feet of the waters which cascade continuously over the rim of the cataract, mesmerised by the magnitude of what is one of the natural wonders of the world. We did the tour through tunnels cut out of living rock which takes one immediately behind the thundering waters and clearly demonstrates the awesome power of nature, and of course we just had to join other tourists on the 'Maid of the Mist', a boat named after an Indian Princess, which cruises to the base of the American Falls before pushing into the basin of the Horseshoe Falls. Curtains of rushing water and a deafening roar engulfs the boat and the spray hits you like tropical rain. The hooded raincoats issued before boarding are not just for fun.

In the evening we took the high speed lift up the Skylon Tower 775 feet above the base of the falls where we enjoyed a fantastic meal in the revolving restaurant. The falls at night should not be missed, lit by powerful xenon lights, the colours change from white to red, green, amber and blue, an unforgettable sight. It was turned midnight when we returned to our hotel in Toronto. It had certainly been a day to remember.

A week in Toronto was enough for me. My wife and I were not great lovers of big cities, besides I had farming friends in the area I wished to visit, Keith and Carol Bacon live at Uxbridge, a 'one horse' settlement 50 miles north of Toronto. The paved road gradually degenerated until it was no more than a wide gravel track heading over the horizon. It made no odds which side of the road I drove on, in fact it was quite safe to drive smack down the centre. There was little traffic. Any approaching vehicles were noticeable five miles ahead, pinpointed clearly by the cloud of dust thrown up! Keith's English wife had been raised on a farm near Basingstoke in Hampshire. I had in the past purchased large white breeding pigs from her father and had known her as a school-girl long before she became a Canadian farmer's wife with four children! We were given a right royal welcome, they didn't often get visitors from the 'old country'.

It was great to get close to nature once more. Swap hard, unforgiving concrete for soft green grass, motor cars for horses, and to be surrounded by cows instead of people. One moved in a lower gear and stopped watching the clock. We got up and went to bed with the sun. On the sixth night of our visit a very severe electric storm struck the area. The heavens opened, I've never known it rain so hard. The thunder cracks were horrendous and continuous lightening flashes lit up the sky. I'm sure the house was struck more than once. All power failed and Keith was concerned for his stock in the barn, but there was little he could do about it. Sleep was impossible so to while away the long night we drank beer and tried to concentrate on a game of cards. With the dawn peace returned, the sun rose and its heat caused steam to rise from the rain soaked earth. The grain crops needed that rain but all hay making was put on hold for a few days. Such are the trials and tribulations of the small family farm in whatever part of the world one lives. Peg and I enjoyed a very pleasant week on a Canadian farm apart from the interruption of the storm. I milked the Pedigree Jersey herd, fed the baby calves and mucked out the hogs. Before the storm I had helped with the hay making which had been in full swing, got thoroughly grubby and built up a suntan.

Our next destination was Ottawa, Canada's capital City. We left the farm early after enjoying a huge 'English' breakfast, the children had been allowed a day off school so that the whole family could wave us goodbye. Carol with generous hospitality packed us enough food and drink to cross a desert. Out of Uxbridge I made for Manchester -yes there is a Manchester in Canada too-then Port Perry on Lake Seagog, a lake of unusual shape with a huge island slap bang in the middle. From this point it is a mere 250 mile journey following the Central Ontario route north-east. We spent four days in the City staying at the luxurious Westin Hotel in the heart of Ottawa. During our stay we took guided tours in the House of Commons and the Speaker's Chamber, we walked the Malls and markets and admired the magnificent parliament building where the changing of the guard takes place similar to the ceremony at London's Buckingham Palace. On the evening of our last night in the city we wined and dined whilst enjoying a romantic cruise along the Rideau Canal and the Ottawa River, but all good things must come to an end. The time had come to leave behind what had become a trusted and reliable friend, our hire car. It had given excellent service over good roads and bad, and we hadn't collided with any other vehicle. I'd even got accustomed to driving on the right-hand side of the road.

My only complaint was that I had spent a small fortune on gas! (petrol)

I just love train journeys and in my opinion there is no better way to see Canada than to cross this vast continent by rail. It is a big country covering seven time zones. Distances have always been a challenge. Canadian National, the largest rail system in

North America spans the country serving every province, from Sydney in Nova Scotia to Vancouver on the West coast, it is a heck of a long way, a train journey that takes five days and four nights if all goes well. When I last did this trip a few years ago the passenger service was down to just the one through train each day. There is of course more than just the one train travelling at any given time, but each one is due to arrive at the same station at the same time each day. Providing notice is given of your intentions you can get off, spend a day, a week, or longer, return and get on the next through train which you know will be there at the same time that you alighted previously. It is not surprising that the journey takes a long time, one doesn't travel very fast, at the best perhaps fifty miles per hour. It is also a single track line, which means that the passenger service has to give priority to freight which necessitates drawing over onto a slip line with a wait of often twenty minutes or more for a freight train to pass. Nevertheless to travel across Canada by CN rail is great fun and a journey never to be forgotten. It is relaxing, one makes new friends, the meals are excellent and above all it is cheap. Having said that I found it not very easy to sleep at night. We had a 'sleeper'. That is how it is optimistically described in the travel brochure. Our sleeper consisted of two bunk beds six feet six inches long but with only four feet head room. I am almost six feet tall, getting undressed and wriggling into a pair of pyjamas is not an easy task in such limited space. After bumping my head a few times I settled down to fitful sleep, but through a long night one gets little peace. The coaches bump, rattle and squeak due to the fact that the train driver is constantly stopping at some lonely station, waiting for the green signal after a mile long freight train has rumbled past or else he is ding-donging on the bell at some unmanned road crossing. We pulled out of Ottawa station at 5.00 pm. I had expected to run quickly into vast tracks of wheat land stretching to the horizon, but this was the first illusion to be shattered. After crossing a small area of farmland, perhaps a hundred miles or so, the remainder of our journey across Ontario was through a land of rock, trees and water. After an excellent meal in the dining car we returned to our bunks to read and hopefully get some sleep. With the dawn I was somewhat surprised to find the forest scenery was still with us, during the night we had travelled north-west through Algonquim Park skirting Timagami Forest reserve and on up around the great lakes. 8:30am September 6th we made yet another stop but this time an hour was allowed for passengers to alight, stretch their legs and 'shop' if they wished. We were at Hornepayne, a small, mainly Indian community which to me seemed in the middle of nowhere. There are approximately four hundred stations on this particular stretch of rail across Canada and although we didn't stop at all of them I got the impression that this estimate is on the low side! Some have interesting names such as Portage du Fort, Fire River, Red Rock, Thunder Bay and Sioux Lookout, an indication of Indian or French connections. Now on our way again it had been fourteen hours since either of us had eaten, my stomach was rumbling, complaining at the lack of attention it was receiving. We decided to explore, make our way through the coaches where fellow passengers were still deep in slumber in their reclining seats. Finally we discovered the dining car. Breakfast was being served, cafeteria style. The aroma was appetising, bacon and eggs, fried or scrambled, beans on toast, sausage and chips, the choice was wide and varied. Neither appealed to us, we could have an English breakfast any old time back home. I'd been brought up on such fare. We chose muffins and maple syrup, a North American speciality and jolly good they are too. Canadians in general are an open, friendly people with no class distinction eager to make conversation and pass the time of day. From what I could gather there were very few, if any English people on board. European tourist don't usually get this far west showing a preference to stay in the big cities back east, or fly over the top to Vancouver. During breakfast the scenery didn't vary very much. Moss covered rocks out of which grew trees and undergrowth almost brushed the sides of the coaches. Occasionally we rumbled over rivers or the narrow neck of a mist shrouded lake on what appeared to be rather rickety wooden bridges. Our route continued through the Nipigon Reserve a beautiful forested area with much wild life and a great lake so well stocked with fish that they really did queue up to bite. A fellow diner informed me of this, with such conviction that I almost believed him.

We continued our journey westwards all through that day and the next long night following the same route that my late father had travelled sixty years previous. The main difference was we travelled in pampered luxury. In his day there were no coaches with reclining seats, air conditioning, comfortable sleeping berths and fully stocked dining carriages! Winnipeg, Canada's gateway to the west and capital of Manitoba. We reached this prairie city of 600,000 people at 10.00 am on the third day. There was a two hour stop over to change crew, refuel and restock the larder. I stepped out of the train, went for a walk down the high street, bought a newspaper and thought of my late father who in his desperate quest for free land had got off the train at Winnipeg and from there had been forced to walk the next 600 miles because the iron horse went no further across the vast prairie that stretched endlessly ahead from now on.

We were on our way once more, but now with a new driver and crew. Was it my imagination or were we going faster? Perhaps it was simply because the line was straight and the prairie flawlessly flat. The scene was of wheat fields and the bare soil of summer fallow as far as the eye could see. Patterned by monstrous tractors, cultivators and combine harvesters. Grain elevators dotted the horizon. The prairies are unforgettable at anytime of the day, but come evening they can be truly awesome with the magic of a blazing big-sky sunset. This was the land that my father had talked so much about with tales that had held me spellbound in my youth. Leaving the province of Manitoba we were now crossing Saskatchewan, known as Canada's bread basket, this Texas sized province is the home of the largest grain farms in the world, with skies bigger, bluer, wider than you have ever imagined. Looking out of the carriage window I tried to grasp my father's thoughts as he, in the company of brothers, sisters, in-laws and my intrepid grand-parents trundled slowly, painfully slowly riding their oxen drawn wagons across what was then a tree-less, road-less land striving for a dream to set up a new home, no comparison with the beautiful Lambourn village of Boxford. Whatever beset them? I knew of course the present owner of Dads old homestead was Chuck Deck but not knowing him in person I could not invite ourselves to stay as his guests. However wishing to sample life for myself on the prairie, crazy though it may seem to many, my wife and I had booked a weeks stay at the 'Rocking W' a 1760 acre grain and beef farm an hours drive out of Watrous, an insignificant township located approximately half-way between Saskatoon and Regina. The train slowed to a stop. "Watrous, anyone for Watrous?" A voiced boomed from somewhere. I opened the carriage door put out the step and touched down on prairie soil for the first time. Peggy handed down our cases then gingerly stepped down herself. Within minutes the train was on it's way, fast disappearing down the track leaving us standing in dejected isolation. What a desolate place to choose for our holiday was a thought that crossed my mind at that moment. "What happens now?" asked my wife apprehensively. "Someone from the farm should have been here to meet us, I expect they will be here soon." I replied, optimistically as always. Five minutes, ten minutes, twenty minutes ticked by, even I was feeling some disquiet. In the far distance a dust cloud rose signalling an approaching vehicle. "That's them coming now I expect." Sure enough a few minutes later a battered, open grain truck pulled up beside us. Out stepped a sun-tanned Canadian farmer. "Sorry I'm late folks, I was out on the swather, clean forgot that you guys were coming. Ross Weisner is the name, welcome to Saskatchewan," he said, pumping my hand vigorously, before turning to Peggy and repeating the gesture, albeit a little more gently!

We had a great time with the Weisner family. In the farm complex was a separate cottage with bathroom, bedroom and a small lounge which we had to ourselves, but meals were taken in the main farmhouse with the family. All this for 55 dollars each per week, a ridiculously tiny sum of money even in those days. Ross and Evelyn had a crowd of kids aged eleven to eighteen at the time. Six of them if I recall correctly which meant that sitting down to meals and joining in with farm life was like home from home. What I quickly learnt was that their farming problems were not that different from ours. A constant battle with crop pests and the weather, low produce prices and perhaps their biggest headache government imposed quotas. With restrictions on the amount of grain they could sell each year, they always had a carry over. They still had wheat in store that had laid in the silo for seven years! "Get another war it will all be wanted," retorted Ross angrily. By the end of the week we had become firm friends of the family. Shelley, aged fifteen at the time, said she would come to England the following Spring to stay on our farm. A promise she kept, much to my daughter Jane's delight.

The time had come for us to move on. Ross drove Peggy and me back to Watrous railway station, at least that is what it is called, in reality it is just marked as a dot on the map. No platform, no ticket office, no waiting room. It is just an excuse for a siding off the main line leading to the brightly painted grain elevators where the wheat crop awaits the freight wagons. Dropping us off in the prairie dust, Ross said, "Sorry I can't stop to see you on your way, must get back to the farm, we are hoping to harvest the last field of wheat today, have a good trip." He revved away in his twenty year old farm truck following a dead-straight road until the dust cloud disappeared with him over the horizon. We sat on our luggage by the side of the rails. There was no one else around, except for half a dozen scrubby children playing amongst some wrecked cars, which had been dumped at the back of a row of single storey wooden houses. Referring to my rail time-table, I read that only one passenger train passed through each day, so providing we hadn't missed it, it would come eventually. I did at one stage put my ear to the rail like we used to as lads, but no distant sound was forthcoming, so we munched a chocolate bar and contemplated how cold it would become if we had to stay out here all night. I supposed I must have nodded off, because on looking up with a start the train was almost upon us. Only when those giant diesel engines and enormous carriages are stopped in front of you, and you are standing at ground level, do you realise how huge they are. Twice the size of rolling stock back in England. We were the only passengers to board and not surprising none got off! A uniformed black porter with dazzling white teeth and a big smile, got off the train placing a footstep on the ground for our convenience. After politely arming Peggy aboard, he placed our suitcases in the carriage. "Please follow me sir, your seats are reserved, I will attend to your luggage later." I didn't offer a gratuity that is something not expected in Canada. My itinerary planned meticulously during the previous eighteen months, allowed time for a stop over at Saskatoon and the northern township of La Ronge. Saskatchewan has two major cities, Regina, capital of the province, known today as Canada's Queen city, and Saskatoon the largest city in the province. My cousin, Henry James Houghton known to his many friends as

Harry, was due to meet us from the train at Saskatoon. In my youth Harry had been my hero, a figure larger than life. I first met my cousin, when he was posted to England with some of the first Canadians to arrive in war-torn Britain, long before the Yanks joined in. To give a measure of the man, Harry joined up as a private and finished the war five years later as a Lt-Col fighting with his unit in the North African battles against Rommel following on through the Italian campaign. Returning to England he landed on the beaches soon after D.Day eventually leading his unit through to Berlin. It had been just a coincidence that when Harry was first posted to England in the early days of war he should be stationed at Reading some twenty miles east of Dymond Farm, my boyhood home. On being granted a weeks leave, what better place to relax than 'down on the farm' in the quiet of the Berkshire countryside with his Aunt Lottie and Uncle Frank. Now at my parents' house we had just three bedrooms. Mum and Dad had the main room of course, whilst my sister and I had a single bed in each of the other two. "Of course we have got room for you Harry, you can muck in with Bert, he doesn't need much room." said my mother gaily. This was true enough. I was in my early teens and slim as a bean pole, but cousin Harry was a big man, broad shouldered and standing six foot four inches in his socks. I lost count of the number of times that I was pushed out of bed when Harry turned over during the night!

After a span of thirty years, we met again at Saskatoon's main railway station. He hadn't changed much, perhaps not looking quite so big in civvies, having hung up his smart uniform and not standing high in size thirteen army boots. Even so, Marion his wife looked puny beside him. What a greeting we received. Kisses from Marion and a bear hug from Harry. Turning to me he said,. "Boy, you've grown up some, filled out a bit too. I understand you've raised a family of seven kids since we last met, and bought yourself two more farms!! My word you two have been busy." "Well, don't forget Harry, it's been half a life-time since we last met." I replied modestly. Greetings over, Harry picked up our cases, two in each hand and marched off talking as he walked. "Now, I intend to take you two to our little abode in La Ronge and for the next week or so we will explore the area, I want to show you our neck of the woods, visit some of my friends in the Indian reservation and also get in some serious fishing." I had the feeling that life with cousin Harry would be planned with military precision. Harry's car was parked just outside the station. I cannot remember what make it was, but this two tonne American monster was eighteen feet long, built to withstand the rigours of the climate and it proved to be very, very greedy on fuel. "You want to drive Bert?" Assuming my answer would be "yes please" Harry opened the driver's seat and beckoned me in. Still bubbling with excitement Harry continued. "It is 250 miles to La Ronge from here, most of the journey over gravel roads, but once we get clear of the City put her in cruise control at 80k, we have to watch the speed limit over here, the cops are hot stuff."

Harry Houghton was La Ronge, La Ronge was Harry Houghton. He had spent a significant part of his life in the area. Mayor of the town for fourteen consecutive years during which time he succeeded in getting the main street paved, successfully harassed authority to finance the building of the area's only hospital, built and managed the only hotel in town and was manager for a time of the nearby mining camp. On top of all those activities he won the hearts and thanks of the local Indian and Metis population, fighting for their lawful rights. He was their "Big White Chief" a Blood Brother of the tribe . That briefly describes my cousin Harry. The eldest son of my father's brother Ralph. Uncle Ralph was the only one of the original Houghton pioneers to prosper in the new land leaving descendants whose hospitality knows no bounds. They have always gone out of their way to make me a welcome visitor. La

Ronge is an interesting locality, isolated, remote, accessible only by plane or the one single gravel road through the bush, with an intermix of people living a completely different lifestyle to that which we enjoy in rural Berkshire. No farming takes place as I know it, the winter-summer temperature variation is too extreme, also there is just no soil to cultivate. Residents lives revolve around fishing, hunting, tour guides, the service industry or just doing nothing at all. La Ronge nestles on the very edge of Lac La Ronge, it is the gateway for hunters and fishermen going even further north. There are no more towns, not even a decent road for hundreds of miles northwards only the bush, muskeg or freshwater lakes, over one hundred thousand of them. In fact the saying goes that if it was possible to fish in a different lake each day, you would not be half-way through your task in a hundred years!

Cousin Harry had built himself a log cabin on one of the many remote islands scattered haphazardly across this huge lake. The highlight of our visit was to be a few days spent in the quiet solitude of the north and at the same time get in some real fishing. I had visions of long hard battles to land trophy-size monsters, casting my thoughts forward to a fishing trip where we would have the deep, cool, crystal-clear lake all to ourselves and where the waters jump with a dozen variety of sport fish. Northern Pike, Walleye, Whitefish and Grayling to name but a few. The afternoon before the great day we fuelled the boat, checked the motor, stacked aboard a weeks provisions and listened intently to the weather reports. No hint was given on the radio of what was on its way from the arctic. "The best made plans of mice and men." So the saying goes. I woke early the next morning anticipating the start of a great adventure, a total new experience was at hand. Yet somehow, something was different. It seemed so quiet, no wind rustled the pine trees of the nearby forest, no noisy early morning traffic out in the street. I pulled back the curtains of Harry's town house, the explanation for the silence stared me in the face. Autumn had turned to winter overnight. Huge snowflakes drifted gently earthwards out of a grey dismal sky. Already snow lay a foot deep. My wife and I were trapped in the unscheduled arrival of a Canadian winter. No way was I going to cast for fish on this vacation. Snow fell all that day continuing through the next night until dawn. When the clouds finally broke, out came the sun. Well if nothing else I must say it all looked very beautiful and of course it wasn't really that cold. When the time came for us to move on, snow ploughs had cleared a way through. In fact, the deep snow only stretched south for a hundred miles or so, but Harry thought it wise not to risk the journey by car. We travelled by coach which made the trip regardless of the weather. Safely back in Saskatoon, Peg and I spent one night at Cousin Merv and Jean Houghton's house. No 610 Rushome Road. Very useful having relatives scattered from coast to coast across this vast land. Noon next day we boarded the Canadian National. Our next stop was to be Edmonton. capital City of Alberta.

The following episode commences back in England.
Prior to this Canadian adventure I had read books, studied maps and spoken in depth to anyone who possessed the slightest knowledge of that country. I have always found that half the fun of a holiday abroad lies in the planning of the itinerary. On a bright spring morning in May 1972, a Tuesday in fact, market day in Salisbury. Driving my loaded cattle truck out of Newbury on the A343 I couldn't fail to notice a well-built young lady standing by the roadside attempting to hitch a lift. Normally I did not stop for hitch-hikers, for one thing, time was money to me, I didn't wish to be late for the sale. But somehow this hitch-hiker was different, her hand signal for a lift was compelling. She had beautiful red hair which fluttered in the breeze, an appealing smile and what was more, attached to her

heavy back-pack a Canadian maple leaf flag. I just couldn't ignore her. That was how I met Linda Smith, a Canadian farmer's daughter. Despite the age difference we were to strike up a friendship destined to last a life-time. In fact in the course of time Linda has become known as my adopted daughter. I stopped, reached across and opened the passenger door. "Where are you heading for young lady?" "Salisbury." she replied. "OK hop up, that is where I'm going." By the time we reached Salisbury I had learnt that her father, Dan Smith farmed at Fawcett some 150 miles north of Edmonton, Alberta, on a large acreage which had taken him a life-time to wrestle from virgin bush. Linda, then just 19 years old had a sister and three brothers. I explained to my young passenger that later in the year when our harvest was completed my wife and I intended to visit Canada. "Oh, that's great, you must come and visit Mom and Dad they'll be sure glad to see you both," she replied with undisguised enthusiasm. In the hustle and bustle of the livestock market we exchanged names and addresses. I helped Linda on with her backpack. Turning round she smiled and said. "Thanks a lot for the lift, sure was kind of you, see you and your wife in Alberta in the fall. Don't forget." With that she was away making for the Cathedral and a sight-seeing tour of the City. Within minutes I was engrossed in the business of the day. But somehow I couldn't forget Linda.

Spring at the farm turned to summer with silage and hay making, finally the corn harvest. Time had come for our trip to Canada.

Of course one is inclined to forget the vast distances involved. On landing at Toronto we had only just started our journey across Canada. When the train eventually stopped at Edmonton we would get off and there, if things went according to plan, would be Linda. My wife was very dubious about the whole thing. "What makes you so certain this girlfriend of yours will be there to meet us?"

"Could be just a fairy story about her father owning a big farm and willing to offer us free board and lodgings for two weeks all on the strength of you giving his daughter a lift to Salisbury in the cattle wagon". "If she is not there what do we do then? We haven't got enough money with us to stay in a hotel for a fortnight and we cannot fly back home until the date shown on our return tickets!" "Now dear, don't worry about it, Linda looks you straight in the eye when she speaks and she has an honest face even if it is freckled."

Linda was there to meet us, I knew she would be. The farm was real, Mom and Dad were real, everything was how she had described it to me. Linda I love you.

The Bear Hunt.

More snow fell whilst Peg and I were relaxing on Dan Smith's farm. The ground froze solid, snow covered the last swathes of unthreshed wheat, the single suckle beef herd required supplementary feeding. Yet a few days later a sudden thaw changed the scene "Would you folk care to collect some cranberries before the birds take them all?" asked Linda's mother one morning. "Sure, we will be pleased to," I replied. "OK, take this basket, go down the dirt track past the corral, carry on until you come to a bridge over the creek, once on the other side cross the summer fallow field until you reach the uncleared bush. In some low-lying ground you will find the wild berries." We enjoyed the pleasant walk to a quiet secluded spot. Having half-filled the container with fruit I ventured deeper into the undergrowth only to disturb a huge black bear. Instinct warned me not to turn and run. The bear ambled off on all fours, stopped, turned and stood upright. We stared at each other for a few seconds then it dropped to the ground and was gone, swallowed up by the trees. We quickly left the scene of confrontation with our meagre collection of fruit having no great desire to dispute ownership of a few berries. On our hurried return to the farmhouse, I reported the incident to Dan thinking that our encounter with a bear would be dismissed as not an unusual event in this neck of the woods. His reaction was unexpected. "Lying up in the berry canes was he?". "He is the so and so that's killed two of my new-born calves recently, we found the carcasses half-eaten, I'll round up the boys and we will go after him." The bear had been condemned without evidence, no witness had seen him at the scene of the alleged crime. It was more than likely that the real culprit was a coyote. In no time at all, Dan, two of his stalwart sons, the hired man and three hurriedly summoned neighbours all armed with rifles or huge sticks were planning the bear's demise. With mounting excitement we left for the woods crammed aboard the three ton farm truck, just as another vehicle raced down the road with reinforcements. The plan of action was to surround the block of bush on three sides then a row of beaters would drive the quarry towards the waiting guns. Now, I don't mind driving a covert to put up a few pheasants back in England but I had no great desire to come face to face in dense undergrowth with a six foot tall black bear in a bad temper, especially as he might be aware that it was me who set him up in the first place. I'm pleased to say that our quarry made a safe exit cleverly doubling back on his tracks and making good his escape where no guns waited. This was probably a blessing in disguise for the waiting marksmen. It is very difficult to hit a moving target with a single rifle bullet, more than likely they would have shot each other!

Our innocent foray to obtain a few edible berries had certainly caused excitement for a while. Back at the farm the hunt party held an inquest into the fiasco, however a few cans of beer soon cured the hunter's depression. Peggy and I kept a low profile secretly pleased that the quarry had made good his escape. After all, from the bear's point of view it was us who had disturbed him in the first place in what he could justly claim was his territory.

Two memorable weeks were spent in the area with Dan Smith and his family. We certainly lived well, Linda's mom proved to be a great cook. Mostly everything we ate was produced on the farm or hunted in the bush. Smoke cured bacon and eggs from free range hens for breakfast, fresh vegetables from the garden and barbecued moose for supper. Even the husky dogs enjoyed a good steak once in a while, and rabbits, there were swarms of them. They were not your Enid Blyton type of bunny. A little brown fellow with big eyes, twitching nose and a white powder -puff tail. These Canadian pests were the big snowshoe rabbit more like a hare, some weighed up to eight pounds. Dan loaned me one of his guns, suitably armed we made for the bush. After a pleasant hour of stalking we had bagged six for the pot. It was to be rabbit pie for lunch during the next couple of days! Dan could skin a rabbit faster-well, almost faster than he could take a tight glove off his hand. A few cuts with the knife, whacks with his axe, and zip off it would come. I've forgotten what he did with the skins. Sadly the time had come for us to move on.

We had one more leg of our trans-Canada journey to complete. This was from Edmonton through the mighty ridge of the Canadian Rockies to Vancouver by C N Rail. Often described as the most fantastic train journey in the world, I'd certainly go along with that, but to give a detailed description of the scenery would fill another book. A few years later on my fourth trip to Canada I hiked and camped in the Rockies with Linda but that is a chapter to come. Three huge diesel engines coupled together are required to pull the train through the mountains, the gradients are so severe. Also more carriages had been attached plus an observation coach. This is a double deck job which allows passengers to relax in comfort and enjoy the panoramic views. Boarding the train at 4.05pm in Edmonton I was disappointed that the scenery would pass unnoticed in the darkness of night travel. I worried unnecessarily, there was still plenty more to come. To be sure of a seat on the observation coach meant an early rise. Peg and I claimed our seats at 5.00 am in good time to see the magnificent sunrise over the snow covered mountain crests as our train made it's way through the Fraser river valley. We were so enthralled by the scenery that we skipped breakfast that morning.

September 27th 1972. Right on schedule after a 5,000 mile journey the train pulled into Vancouver central station. Struggling along the platform with our luggage, I stopped at the lead locomotive, gave the huge monster a friendly tap, took a photograph for posterity and shouted thanks to the driver who had opened the side window of his cab for a breath of fresh of air. "Have a nice day," he replied with a smile. Once out of the station we joined a small queue for the first available taxi. It was at this point in time that I realised that we were now within walking distance of the Georgia Strait. An ambition achieved, I had crossed the vast continent from east to west, ocean to ocean, albeit in a certain amount of luxury, all thanks to those pioneers who had surveyed and finally built a rail-line through such inhospitable terrain. Vancouver, with the Pacific Ocean at its feet and rugged coastal mountains as backdrop is acknowledged as one of the world's most beautiful cities. We spent a week at Hotel Vancouver relaxing in a double room with a king-size bed and every luxury one could imagine for just thirty-two dollars a night. An unbelievable pittance by today's standards, some twenty years later. The days flashed by, we had an active week of sight-seeing. Vancouver, Canada's third largest city is a place to browse fashionable shops, linger in side-walk cafes, lunch on a pier or have dinner on a mountain top. We enjoyed the colourful sights of Chinatown, second only in size to San Francisco. We strolled through Stanley Park, a thousand acres of urban forest, a park of many trails, huge Douglas Firs and fantastically carved Totem poles. Just minutes away is Lions Gate Bridge. We joined other tourists to walk across the swaying suspension bridge, which spans the gorge of the Capilano river, finally riding on the 'Super Skyride' tramway to the top of Grouse Mountain which gives a breathtaking view of the entire city and coastline. However, I had to admit, that of late I hadn't been giving much thought to my farm back in 'Beautiful Berkshire'. My home and livelihood was in the hands of my young, inexperienced family and our hard working stock lady Dora Jerome. Eventually on our safe return we received a wonderful home-coming reception. The farm was still intact, there had been no major disasters and the bank had not foreclosed. Despite my misgivings, it had been proved to me that no one is indispensable. Once we recovered from 'jet-lag', my wife and I were soon back into the swing of things, little had changed 'down on the farm.'

1976 was a catastrophic year for myself and family. My dear wife who had stood by me through good times and bad for the last thirty years, died suddenly at the farmhouse on January 17th 1976. At the time she was doing nothing more strenuous than enjoying a cup of tea with the younger members of the family. This disaster happened just as she was beginning to pursue more leisure activities after a quarter of a century rearing seven children. I was grateful that at least we had both enjoyed a fantastic holiday in Canada a few years before. Farm life continued, it has to. The cows still need milking twice each day, all the livestock must be fed and one's children got to school on time.

The following year an invitation to a wedding and reception came by post. Dan Smith's second daughter Janet was to married in Westlock, Alberta. Linda wrote a letter too, insisting that I should accept. On no account would she take no for an answer. "Your daughter Jane will come with you for company." she added. Unbeknown to me, my kids held a conference, then they got me round the table. "Course you must go Dad, get you out of yourself, you've got to look to the future, life goes on. We can run this farm and look after ourselves. We've proved that before remember?" Jane and I went to Canada.

My daughter Jane and I had a memorable time on this my second trip to Canada. It was indeed a grand wedding and of course I saw Linda again.

My third visit to Canada.

This was with my son Richard. What an adventure that turned out to be! It all started with an invitation from my cousin Harry Houghton and his wife Marion. They were planning a big family reunion to celebrate their 50th wedding anniversary in Prince Albert, Saskatchewan. Richard and I were to represent the English members of the Houghton clan. Flying out from Heathrow we landed in Toronto some eight hours later where we were met by Lynn Houghton, a female cousin of mine who at that time held high rank in the Canadian Army. High enough up the promotional ladder to fly her own plane and pull a few administration strings when necessary. The forthcoming anniversary celebrations were two weeks ahead, in the meantime we would be guests of the armed forces and reside with Lynn in the Officer's quarters at Camp Bordon, fifty miles or so out of Toronto. During the next couple of weeks Richard and I explored the surrounding countryside. When Lynn couldn't come with us a car was provided at Government expense. On one occasion when a long drive was planned to visit Niagara Falls, I just happened to mention to Lynn that it would be nice to have food and drink for a picnic en route. "Call at the canteen on your way out. I will get food and drink provided," said Lynn confidently. Well, bless my newly issued army boots. Didn't the cook know that there was only two of us? Enough food and drink had been provided to maintain a small reconnaissance patrol! When we did set out our picnic at Niagara, the goodies covered a table all of eight feet long. "Get the camera Richard, we must take a picture of this lot to show our family back home or they will never believe us."

Lynn had a month's leave due which was timed to coincide with her parent's anniversary celebrations and also leave ample time to lead an expedition down the Churchill River. "Would Richard and yourself like to tag along?" "It will mean roughing it a bit, but it should prove to be an adventurous trip." This was an unexpected opportunity to visit the real Canada, the unpolluted, unpopulated north. We jumped at the chance.

After two weeks in a military camp even without joining in the square bashing, Richard had come to the conclusion that the regimental lifestyle of the army was not for him, and both of us were only too pleased to board Lynn's plane and be personally flown half-way across the continent to Prince Albert. Crossing the Great Lakes in a small plane was an eye-opener, especially passing over Lake Superior. We seemed to be flying over water for hours, for a long spell there was no sight of land in either direction. I couldn't believe that it was only a lake and not open sea. Safely in Prince Albert cousin Harry assumed control. He had reserved rooms in a plush hotel for all long distance guests. "Leave all the financial arrangements to me, just get on and enjoy yourselves," he said with gay abandonment. "Oh, and by the way Bert and Richard, you will be having a working breakfast with me and The Right Honourable John George Diefenbaker, ex Conservative Prime Minister of Canada tomorrow morning, he is an old friend of mine. 8.00 am sharp in the hotel's main dining room. Don't be late."

Note:- In the General Election of June 10th 1957 the Conservative Party won the largest number of seats in the 23rd Parliament and John Diefenbaker was called on as Prime Minister of Canada and was sworn in office on June 21st 1957. His government was re-elected on March 31st 1958 and on

June 18th 1962. In the general election of April 8th 1963, the progressive Conservative Party reverted to the role of opposition and John Diefenbaker assumed the office of Leader of Her Majesty's Loyal Opposition in the House of Commons, from which position he resigned on September 25th 1967.

The celebration of Harry and Marion's happy event started with a slap-up lunch in the Canadian Legion Hall, to be followed by the usual after dinner speeches which continued through most of the after-noon. After a short break for revellers to get second breath, round two continued until the early hours of the following day. Once the clock past midnight the country and western live band really got going with a swing. At one stage my son Richard was given the whole dance floor to whirl his lissom Red Indian dance partner round the room. Fifteen minutes later with the applauding spectators threatening to bring down the roof, the pair collapsed in sheer exhaustion. Until then I hadn't realised my son was such an entertainer. No one rose very early or very sober the next day, yet somehow most of the clan met in the country garden of one of Harry's many friends. It is seldom possible to get such a large family together, and was probably the only time that I will ever get to meet all my Canadian cousins in one group. A quick count confirmed that there were thirty-seven of them, although I admit that there were some two or three times removed. It is said of course that blood is thicker than water and it amazed me the family characteristics we shared, even though living thousands of miles apart.

Two days later Richard and I departed from Prince Albert accompanied by Lynn, Merv and his wife Jean. We were to meet up with Gary Houghton and a few of his venturesome acquaintances at La Ronge, that small township on the western bank of Lac La Ronge. From this point we had planned to make our way by boat out to Merv's cabin on Peanut Island (later to be officially renamed Houghton Island), and from then on Lynn was to lead our small party on an adventure trip down the Churchill river until we reached the Nistowiak Falls. Saskatchewan's north is an endless maze of waterways, lakes, streams and churning, cascading rivers like the mighty Churchill, and scenery that can leave one breathless. Crossing the lake by boat takes anything up to three hours depending on conditions, in open areas the water can be turbulent. It is essential to know the lake because there are many dangerous reefs which can tear the bottom out of your boat, but Richard and I were in good hands. Lynn's knowledge of this vast area of fresh water was second to none. There were eight of us in the party, now crammed into two small motor boats one of which was towing an unsinkable paddleboat. One boat belonged to the Houghton's, the other one had been hired and it was this last one that began to play up. It did make the crossing-just, but the engine packed up completely on the return journey causing much consternation. On the north side of the Lake the water flows out, through a deep rocky gorge. This is the continuation of the Churchill which eventually discharges it's water into Hudson Bay. After an uneventful crossing of the lake the boats were secured at this point. We continued down river in the unsinkable craft. At least the makers claimed it couldn't sink, but we were to find out that it could tip over! But first things first. After the lake crossing, our leader suggested that we 'boiled the billy'. A fire was lit on a rocky ledge well clear of the bush. Black coffee, toast and beans, the standard fare of North American outdoor life. It had been a long time since we had eaten, this simple meal was enjoyed with great gusto. The only thing that dampened our spirits where the inescapable mosquitoes, not even the smoke of the fire kept them clear. Their appetite for English blood was insatiable. The first two miles after it leaves Lac La Ronge, the Churchill cuts through a deep gorge which necessitates a long portage. Fortunately a rail line has been built through the bush to enable river travellers to transport their gear on bogie wheels. Since it is mostly downhill, one can climb aboard and ride, but it is not much fun on the return journey! Once clear of the gorge the river widens continuing it's tortuous course north-eastwards at a quieter pace for many miles, but after a while in the distance could be heard the churning of rushing water. 500metres downstream, on rounding a sharp left-hand bend of the river, our speed increased dramatically, now we were white-water rafting at Potter Rapids on the Churchill. More by luck than skill we survived some very rough water and dangerous looking rocks. A far cry from punting sedately down the Isis at Oxford with my daughter Jane on a summer's afternoon. Late in the day we reached our objective, very wet and physically exhausted. At the base of these imposing falls a few of the more energetic members of the party tried their hand at fishing. I remember Richard got quite a catch of Walleye. Supper that evening was a pleasant change from beans on toast!! The return journey back to the lake two days later was a tiring and difficult one. We portaged more than we paddled but it had been an adventure to remember. Unfortunately our problems were not over by any means. We still had to make the return journey across the lake, no big deal with two sound boats, but the hired craft refused to start despite the engine being partly dismantled by the 'mechanics' in the party. We had no radio, were 50 miles from civilisation and food was running low. One consolation at least the water of the lake is drinkable and fish are plentiful! It appeared that we had two choices, the serviceable boat could cross the lake and summons help, alternatively if we could make it to a certain nearby island which Lynn remembered was inhabited by a lone trapper who apparently was the proud owner of a two way radio, rescue could be organised. We chose the latter. Splitting the party into both boats, with the serviceable craft towing the loaded broken down boat, we made it to the trapper's island. From there a radio call swiftly brought a float plane to lift six of our party back to base. Lynn insisted that Richard and myself flew back. She and one other member of the party would bring back the family boat leaving the other one for collection at a later date. When all were on board, the plane was overcrowded, the weather foul and visibility poor. This made for a rough flight back to La Ronge, but I had clocked up another first. It was the first time I had flown in a plane that could only land on water. Thus ended that particular adventure for two greenhorns from England.

On two more occasions I crossed Canada from coast to coast travelling by Canadian National Railways. One must remember that this is a big country covering seven time zones. Distances have always been a challenge to the traveller. Setting out from Toronto one first crosses the vast province of Ontario then the prairie states of Manitoba, Saskatchewan and Alberta on and on through the mighty ridge of the Rockies to Vancouver, where the sun sets on Canada every evening. From here on in my story I intend to pick out just the highlights of my travels of North America, but firstly I must mention that it was on one of these journeys that I finally made it to my father's homestead, for myself a nostalgic occasion, but this story is recorded in my second book "Just more of the Berkshire Farmer".

On this my fourth visit to Canada, I was accompanied by my second wife Ruth and my 16 year old daughter Bobby. At one time I had planned to take all my children to Canada, but as things turned out I took just three of them, one at a time I should add. Bobby is not my youngest daughter's real name. She was christened Ruth Mary, but being the baby of the family with five older brothers to contend with, she turned out to be a real tom-boy. She rarely played with dolls and such like, but climbed trees, rode boisterous horses, played aggressive

Bobby drives the combine harvester. Big Easton. Dymond Farm

football, even drove the combine harvester when only 13 years of age and possessed a short-temper. She got her nickname from the fact that she always wore a silly woolly hat with a red bobble. She was seldom seen without it, even wore it in bed!

After yet another trans-Canada journey we got off the train at Edmonton to be met once more by Linda, who by now had acquired a husband, Bryan and a son at that time age 6. Hugs and kisses over, our luggage was stacked in the back of the Four-by-Four Dormobile. We were then driven to their new house in Westlock, a home that they took great pride in, especially since it had been built mainly by Bryan and Linda's own labour. Our young hosts had arranged their annual holiday to coincide with our visit. We were to be allowed two days rest before making for the mountains. They had no intention of letting us laze in the Autumn sunshine, drink, eat to excess and just sleep it off. Nothing so mundane for the English visitors. In due course two large tents were packed aboard our transport, plus hiking gear, ground sheets, sleeping bags, and ample food supplies for a ten day trek in the Rockies. I must record here that on the first stage of this trip we were joined by Ruth's cousin Vivien who lives on the outskirts of Calgary, a relative that Ruth hadn't seen for many years. The adventure proper commenced high in the mountains with two days for the party to acclimatise, camping by the side of a fast flowing ice-cold river. During this short period Bryan taught us campcraft, navigation, survival techniques and most important, how to work together as a team. He also insisted we practised 'bear-hanging'. This was to hang all our food high in the air between trees and away from our tents to stop bears being attracted to us. "You have to hang toiletries too, because bears love tooth paste," chipped in Linda with a smile. "There are also racoons, chipmunks, caribou and coyotes around," she continued. "I'm getting scared before we start," I confessed. Really of course there was no need to get worried, black bears and the more dangerous grizzlies will not generally come into one's campsite unless they are really hungry, and will only attack if they feel threatened. On the morning of departure spirits ran high and adrenaline flowed, this trek into the wilderness was something that Ruth and I could relate to our grandchildren on our return. With back packs heavy on our shoulders we were on our way. The first day took in beautiful Lake Louise and the Angel Glacier. The second day we followed the tortuous course of the Athabatca River deep in the mountains to Peyto Lake, Emerald Lake and many others which share the same amazing colour, a true opaque turquoise, the result of glacial till or rock flour particles reflecting the blue/green spectrum of light. The following day took us to Moraine Lake in the isolated valley of Ten Peaks. Each day we climbed higher, I must admit, by now the altitude was having its effect on Ruth and me, the younger members of the party experienced no problem. Finally, hiking through an August snowstorm we crossed Senitel Pass at 8,500 feet. Dropping to lower levels on the other side of the pass the wind abated and snow turned to rain, yet if given a choice I think I prefer the white stuff, you can brush it off and you don't get so wet. We pitched camp that night by the rapids of a turbulent stream where we took a well earned rest for a couple of days. Each morning we were up and around at sun-up. There is something special about a Rocky Mountain dawn. The sun creeping over the peaks, the freshness in the air. Just something you can't buy in the city for a thousand dollar bill. Bryan lit up a small Calor gas cooker and Linda cooked the breakfast. Actually she can stir up a fair pan of porridge. It wasn't a bad breakfast of porridge, bacon, eggs and coffee, I've known worse in my early camping days. On day ten we broke camp and returned to Bryan's Oldsmobile which had been left in a long term car park. During the next few days we toured the area on wheels. The great beauty of travel in the Rocky mountains is the ease with which you can lose everybody and yourself in some of the most splendid country in the world. One of our best mornings was spent sitting by a swamp ten minutes walk from the main highway, watching a family of beavers bustling round their lodge. Cruising slowly, well off the beaten track, we kept the binoculars handy and in this way we saw a black bear and her cub lumbering off into the pines. Later, on entering a remote valley, Linda gave an excited cry. "Look, right up there on that rocky outcrop." Following the line of her outstretched hand, I could see nothing to get excited about, nor could any of my companions, until something moved and now we saw them. A bunch of bighorn sheep standing on a bluff looking down their Roman noses at us. Finally Bryan drove us to the Athabasca Glacier, largest icefield south of the Arctic Circle, but it could well have been Blenheim Palace or Windsor Castle with its crammed coach park and camera clicking tourists. We were told that on a good day some 4,000 people are snow-coached onto the 1,000 foot thick ice-and they do say that if you drink the glacier's melt-water you will never grow old. But in my case perhaps it was too late, I was already sixty years old at the time.

1992. Canada bound once more.
On this my fifth trip to Canada, I was to travel further north than ever before. Dianne Scoles, who lived at that time with her husband Ted and six grown up children in the City of Thompson, Northern Manitoba is the daughter of my late cousin Frank Houghton. She had always kept in touch with her English relatives and in frequent letters had complained bitterly that despite an open invitation I had never managed even a brief social call, but one must remember that it is not always practical to cross the Atlantic then to transport oneself two or three thousand miles across often difficult terrain, just to drop in for a cup of tea! Yet, rather rashly I promised Dianne that on this trip, by hook or by crook I would spend a few weeks with the Scoles.

Ruth and I took a direct flight from Heathrow to Winnipeg, the nearest main airport to Thompson. I never tire of flying over Greenland at 37,000 feet to look down on that white, frozen barren land without a speck of green. Another drink, yet another meal and one is on the long haul across the desolate wastes of the North West Territories before dropping gently down to our destination, Winnipeg, capital city of Manitoba. We were met at the airport by Dianne's husband, Ted. To save us the hassle of travelling to Thompson by public transport he had popped down by car to collect us. A mere 800 miles each way! Ted had wisely booked a hotel room for the night in Winnipeg explaining to us that if we all had a good night's rest an early start could be made next morning. Even then it would be too long a journey to complete in one day. His intention was that we kipped down for the night at a log cabin on the shore of Clearwater Lake, the summer home of Margie Houghton, Dianne's widowed mother.

Manitoba, Canada's heartland province is a land of interesting people and varied scenery. In the far north which we intended to visit there are evergreen forests covering thousands of square miles as well as uncountable rivers, numberless lakes and vast areas of treeless tundra. The next day, true to form, the sun shone out of a cloudless sky. We were clear of Winnipeg's built-up area by 8.00 am heading west on the Trans-Canada Highway as far as Portage La Prairie. At this point we left the highway travelling north-west on the long haul off the western shore of Lake Winninpegosis. On and on we seem to drive, but finally reached the log cabin on Clear Water Lake where we spent the night. Word of our approach had preceded us, Margie had made ready for her visitors and had prepared an evening meal that would have done justice to Royalty. I wish we could have stayed longer in this beautiful spot, but the next day we continued on our long journey. Late on the second day we were met by my jovial cousin at No 4 Hillside Crescent, Thompson, Canada's newest city, at that time barely twenty-five years old. It is built on the banks of the Burntwood River which flows north-west until reaching Hudson Bay. What a welcome Ruth and I received. I believe I am correct in claiming that we were the first of their English relatives ever to make the long journey from the old country and reach so far north. Ted and Dianne had at that time six teenage children, four of them their own and two were adopted, Ernie and Donna, both of native Indian blood. Unfortunately Donna was to perish, caught in the open at night in a snow blizzard, Canadian winter's can be cruel and must not be treated lightly.

Whilst on this holiday we managed to get in some fantastic fishing on nearby lakes. It maybe an exaggeration to say that the fish line up to bite in Manitoba, but thousands of anglers vow that's exactly what happens. We quickly caught the spirit of the north country. The lakes are cool, deep and inviting, they act as a tonic to the pressures of big city life and with either Ted or Ernie in charge of the boat we had the advantage of arguably, the most experienced guides in the province. Then there is the challenge of the fishing itself, of battles with a Northern Pike on the end of your line, a fish that is considered one of the fiercest and most thrilling of all freshwater game fish. On one occasion Ruth was sure she'd hooked some gigantic monster of the deep as she strained to pull it into the boat. "Help, help me Ted," she cried as the trophy sized catch began to pull the boat along. With Ted's help the fish was pulled close enough to capture in the net. It was a monster, a real beauty and we dined well that evening. The camera proved that it was not a tall tale of the one that got away!

Dianne's husband Ted Scoles was at the time area manager for a telephone company, covering the whole of Northern Manitoba. "I have a business trip coming up which will take Dianne and myself to Churchill, would you two like to tag along?" he enquired. Now I'm not the sort of person to miss a chance like that, after all Churchill, the only town of any size on Hudson Bay, is the only place in the world for viewing Polar Bears in the wild in substantial numbers, but of course it was going to be quite an adventure to get there, there are no roads to Churchill. You either go by train or take a float-plane. The train travels through a land of unlimited forest, for over 500 miles on a rail line built in the last century, mainly to transport prairie grown wheat to the only port in Hudson Bay.

The once-a-day passenger train pulled out of Thompson at 6.00

pm, plunging almost immediately into a vast uninhabited land of lakes, muskeg and evergreen forest covering thousands of square miles. The four of us were sharing a sleeping cabin which was so designed that once the bunk beds were stacked away we could enjoy the comfort of a small lounge. After a meal in the dining carriage, we spent a long evening playing poker, but not for large stakes, I should add! All through the night the train trundled northwards as I slept fitfully. Looking out of my carriage window at 7.00 am the sun was already high in the sky, nights are short in this part of the world at this time of year. The scene that met my eye had changed completely from the day before. The dense stands of evergreen and deciduous trees had thinned out, not only were they far apart, but also none of them stood more than six feet high whilst some were like bonsai trees just one or two feet tall, yet probably over hundred years old. Long before we got to Churchill even these stunted specimens disappeared completely, we had reached the frozen sub-arctic, the Tundra.

The town of Churchill was perhaps how I had imagined it to be, a hotchpotch of wooden houses, a few shops, a bank or two and surprise, surprise a super market built in a prominent position on the only cross-roads in town, and the shoppers coming out through the automatic doors with laden trolleys were mainly Eskimo women! Now, this scene completely shattered my vision of the frozen waste-land of northern Canada. Ruth and I had travelled hundreds of miles almost to Eskimo Point on the shores of Hudson Bay, expecting to view polar bears in the wild and Eskimo's living off the land as their forebears had, since time immemorial. The only Eskimos we saw were getting their necessaries of life from the local supermarket just like we do back home. And as for polar bears the only ones we saw were those in prison!! A massive building on the edge of town, the interior divided into separate re-inforced concrete pens with strong iron gates and a high

At the old Fortress Hudson Bay.

walkway above for feeding the occupants. Apparently any bears wandering into the town in search of food are shot by the guards with a tranquilliser gun, once unconscious they are transported to the prison awaiting transport far away from habitation. Once the Hudson Bay freezes over in late October, the bears disappear almost overnight heading for those rich seal-hunting areas on the pack ice.

We enjoyed our stay in Churchill, the locals are a unique community of warm hearted people and in the short summers the surrounding countryside brings a rich variety of red, purple, yellow and white carpet of Tundra flowers.

On a wilderness encounter aboard a ramshackle bus we saw ringed and bearded seals frolicking on the banks of the Churchill River and on taking a boat trip into the estuary, we had a close up view of the Beluga whales which move in and out with the changing tides to feed and raise their young in the mouth of the Churchill and the Bay. The only thing that marred our pleasure in the Hudson Bay area were the voracious mosquitoes craving our blood, luckily we were equipped with bug-jackets which offered some protection.

Back once more in the City of Thompson we enjoyed a few days rest from our travels before setting off to La Ronge. Ted kindly volunteered to transport Ruth, myself and our luggage to our destination. Now that in itself *is* some trip. "It is not just down the road." Travelling west, mostly on unpaved roads it took us two days of hard driving. We stopped for the night and a meal in Flin Flon, a mining town carved out of the bush and sitting astride the Manitoba/Saskatchewan border 397km from Thompson. I didn't like the town, it struck me as a very unhealthy place to live. The effect of acid rain from the chemical works has destroyed vast areas of the surrounding forest. We couldn't leave the place fast enough, but some people have to do these jobs I suppose. I'd rather milk cows and feed and muck out pigs, at least the smells are natural!

Back in La Ronge we were met by Merv and Jean and whisked across the lake in a speed boat to dock on Houghton Island, where we stayed in the log cabin and spent a leisurely week fishing, canoeing and doing just nothing at all. I could easily have spent a month there, but all too soon we took our leave heading south for Saskatoon, where we caught the train for Vancouver.

A few pleasant days were spent in this beautiful city before we took the ferry to Nanaimo on Vancouver Island, where we visited yet another of my cousins. A few days later we left for Victoria, to catch the plane to Edmonton, transferring to a continental jet. In 9 hours we were back once more at Heathrow and the end of yet another adventurous holiday.

Around the World in Eighty Days

As many of you know Phileas Fogg accomplished this feat in the latter years of the nineteenth century. In doing so he won a wager of twenty thousand pounds, a huge sum in those days. At the end of his journey the poor man thought he had lost the bet having taken a few hours more than eighty days but in fact he had only taken 79 days. The cause of his error was simple. Phileas Fogg, had, without suspecting it, gained one day on his journey, and this, merely because he had travelled constantly eastward; he would on the contrary, have lost a day had he gone the other way round! On the journey eastwards he had gone towards the sun, and the days therefore diminished for him as many times four minutes as he crossed degrees on the circumference of the earth, and these three hundred and sixty degrees, multiplied by four minutes, give precisely twenty-four hours- that is, the day unconsciously gained. In other words, while Fogg, going eastwards saw the sun pass the meridian eighty times, his associates in England only saw it pass the meridian seventy-nine times. He had won his bet.

Ruth and I set out to circumnavigate the world at 8 pm on November 13th 1982 sailing out of Southampton water on the

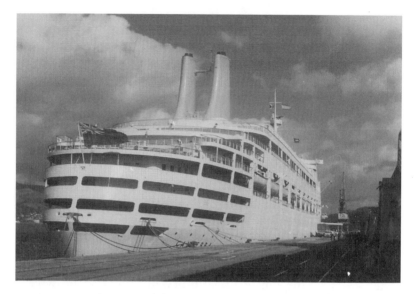

Canberra our floating home for the world cruise

cruise ship Canberra. We travelled westwards and our journey round the world was to take us just about the same number of days as Phileas Fogg had taken about 100 years previously. One big difference was that in our case we were not out to diminish his achievement or to break any other record and having sailed to New Zealand in forty days we spent the next forty days in that beautiful country before completing the second half of our journey home on a 747 jet plane. Though in many ways not as dramatic as Fogg's adventures our trip was not uneventful. Six weeks on a boat, first across the Atlantic then the vast Pacific Ocean is not without its ups and downs. To leave Southampton on a big liner is a very moving occasion. It is not just another cruise for the affluent society, a luxury binge for the elderly. On board were many couples, family groups and a few just getting away from it all. Emigrants to distant lands, a new life, leaving behind friends, relatives or even enemies, maybe for many years or for good. My step-daughter Sue, her first husband Charles, their children Edward and Catherine, and also my cousins Jack and Shirley Perris were allowed on board until 7.30 pm. Then after being ushered ashore they waited on the quay side to watch us leave. The colourful band of the Royal Marines struck up giving a stirring send-off with appropriate tunes like "Life on the ocean wave" and "Now we are sailing." Like umbilical cords, coloured streamers briefly held departing families to relatives and friends ashore. A very happy occasion but also a sad one for many leaving England behind for years or even a lifetime. Only as the paper streamers start to snap does one realise that at last this great ship is on her way.

Now there was no turning back, this Berkshire Farmer had committed himself and his wife to a long spell of life at sea. We made our way to the inside cabin reserved for us on "B" deck grateful to find that our suitcases had miraculously arrived before us, so too had a bouquet of flowers and a bottle of champagne. Some kind person somewhere had thought of us. First things first, we sampled the bubbly, whilst at the same time took stock of our tiny cell-like cabin. With no porthole one has to rely completely on artificial light, also you get no sense of movement with no outside view, a berth with a porthole is far superior but I'd had to study cost. Next we unpacked our suitcases which were in imminent danger of bursting open unless attended to, an assorted variety of winter and summer clothes strewed the cabin, half of which would in due course prove to be completely unnecessary and only brought along for the ride! Changing into evening dress we somehow found our way to the Atlantic restaurant and after being introduced to our future dining companions enjoyed our first meal at sea. By now Canberra was sailing sedately down the English Channel. The captain and first officers were well aware of what weather conditions lay ahead, it was their job to know, but most of the passengers, including Ruth and I were blissfully unaware of what the Atlantic Ocean can throw at those who dare to venture on it. The gale struck with unbelievable force in the early hours. It lasted all next day, through the following night and well into the second day. Visibility even in day time seemed almost nil, thank goodness for radar! Rain was driven horizontally by the howling gale, mountainous seas caused the ship to dip down one great trough then up over the next wave sending sea water cascading over promenade deck which is normally 50 feet or more above the water line. That first meal which we had enjoyed so much didn't stay down for long, what a waste of good food that proved to be! For the next three days we were both terribly sea sick, the only relief was got was by staying in our bunks trying to roll with the ship. We had been told that the Canberra had stabilisers and didn't roll, don't believe it, it does in those seas. Even the piano was tossed across the dance floor with half the band and most of the few brave dancers. The captain later admitted that even whilst Canberra was taking part in the Falklands war he had never experienced such atrocious weather. We asked ourselves, "What have we done leaving our beautiful, steadfast valley, the comfort of Mousefield Farmhouse with our roaring log fires and all our friendly animals?" All in exchange for this mad, mad world where you cannot keep a meal down and you wish that you could curl up and die. At the height of the storm Canberra answered a "May-Day" call from a ship in distress 160 miles north of our position, our captain immediately altered course whilst at the same time realising it would take six hours to reach the other ship. After a few hours a radio message confirmed that another ship in the vicinity had picked up survivors, so Canberra changed course again and increased speed to try and make up lost time. The sea was still rough but abating. What a long way it is across the Southern Atlantic.

November 19th 1982 7.00 am

Great excitement amongst early morning strollers on the promenade deck. That smudge on the horizon was not a low cloud but our first sight of land for almost a week. The Bermudas was our first port of call and now the 22 square mile area of volcanic islands were coming up fast. The ship anchored in Grassey Bay near the entrance to the Great Sound and from there passengers were quickly landed ashore by local tender at the terminal in Hamilton, a minor trip of thirty minutes.

My first steps on land after a week at sea were definitely unsteady. I could have sworn that the island was not a mountain top firmly attached to the ocean floor but somehow just a huge floating raft. It was only when I eventually returned to the ship that I felt at ease. I had become a sailor in a very short time! We spent a full day on the island, first a visit to the crystal caves then onto the perfume factory where one is leisurely escorted through a building with the most aromatic smells. At the end of the tour the only exit proved to be through the shop where free-spending tourists are conveniently offered perfume at "factory prices."

The afternoon was taken up by watching the Dolphin show. These very intelligent animals always give pleasure with their skills in the water, despite half the audience getting a thorough soaking. Dinner was at 7 pm in the Clay House Inn, which also doubles as a night club, where we were entertained in spectacular fashion by Limbo dancers and the Trinidad Steel Band. It had turned midnight when the last of the revellers finally returned to the Canberra, now a welcome blaze of coloured lights as she proudly rode at anchor. The magnificent flagship of the P&O Cruise line.

November 20th – Next day

According to my log of the cruise we weighed anchor at 7.32 am and proceeded southwards from Grassey Bay. Once clear of Bermuda we set a south-west by westerly course towards Florida. Between Bermuda and Port Everglades the distance steamed was 934 nautical miles at an average speed of 20.09 knots. On this crossing the weather had been perfect, the sea mirror-like with a gentle breeze off-shore and a day-time temperature of 80 degrees. F. I was beginning to enjoy myself. For relaxation I spent many hours writing script for my autobiography and to work up an appetite for the evening meal I had joined the cricket team. Passengers v Crew. Yes, one can play cricket on board ship, with slightly different rules than those ashore but nevertheless a very energetic sport. I note from my diary that we scored 75 runs against the crews' reply of 143. My contribution was to claim one wicket and score just 8 runs, but I held my own in the Cricketer's bar after the game. Unknown to me, instead of cheering on the passengers' side Ruth had slipped away to join a drinks party with the Captain, D.J. Scott-Mason CBE. RD. RNR.

November 22nd – Dawn.
Dead ahead lay the unforgettable sky-line of Miami. Two hours later we sailed into Port Everglades to dock at 9.00 am. Port Everglades lies within the city limits of Fort Lauderdale and is approximately 25 miles north of Miami. Warmed in winter by the Gulf Stream and cooled in summer by continuous, refreshing sea breezes it has a remarkable even climate, a play ground not only for Americans but the rest of the world. Once ashore Ruth and I were unanimous in deciding that our primary interest lay in wildlife. Beaches, city shops and crowds of people took second place. We joined a safari tour to lion country where we had the opportunity to film big game imported and set free on plains similar to the African Savannah. Our visit to Miami had been all too short, but a flying visit is perhaps better than not at all. Back to our temporary floating home, that big white

ship that graces the horizon wherever she goes, a ship whose outline makes you feel excited, just to see her, riding there at anchor, waiting just for you and capable of wafting you from one romantic place to another.

The next two days and nights were spent crossing the Caribbean Sea. We altered course round Cape Maysi on the western extremity of Cuba, entered the Windward Passage before sailing on a south-south westerly course towards Cristobal our next port of call. 4.00 pm November 25. The day was almost gone when we finally tied up at No. 8 Pier alongside the Royal Yacht Britannia. We did go ashore for a few hours, just time for a very interesting meal and entertainment by the Panamanian Folklore Dancers. Back to the ship at a very late hour, just time to snatch a few hours sleep before sailing with the tide at 6.00 am. The choice before our Captain was to take Canberra through the Panama Canal and into the Pacific at the cost of £25,620 toll or cruise right round the tip of South America which would probably cost a lot more money and certainly extend the journey. In any case I had no desire to tempt providence with a trip south of the Falkland Islands and through stormy Drake Passage!!

The transit of the Panama Canal was an unforgettable voyage. At this early hour most of the ships passengers were still in their bunks or state room beds sleeping off the previous nights banquet. With the prospect of a unique experience Ruth and I rose early, skipped breakfast and made our way to the observation deck. The first lock system is one and a fifth miles long, each lock one thousand feet from end to end and one hundred and ten feet wide. Since Canberra is 102'6" wide at the water line this allows just 3'3" each side to spare. As the ship slowly approached the first lock I was positive that no way could we pass through that narrow strip of water. The ship looks too gigantic, the lock so small. It is of course an optical illusion. From our vantage point the ship appears to be so wide, far wider than the lock but way down below at the water line there is just inches to spare. Our pilot didn't even scratch the paintwork! Big ships don't use their own power but are pulled through by "Mules". No, not the long eared variety but powerful diesel locomotives which run on rails and are assisted in their mammoth task by a cog wheel engaging a centre rail. If the reader is interested in statistics, the first ship passed through in 1914. In those days just 5 ships a day, now something like 40 plus. 40,000 men died in the Canal's construction through an area that was once the most disease ridden spot on earth. Something which I could understand because the day we passed through, it was terribly hot and humid. More like being in a sauna than on board ship. The first system of locks called the Gatum locks takes ships through and into the man-made Gatum Lake if you are travelling west-wards. Shortly after, one enters the Guya Cut which is 9 miles long. The magnitude of the project will be better appreciated when it is realised that the range of hills through which the canal was cut was 276 feet above sea-level. It was this nine mile stretch of the canal that the major part of the work was concentrated. In addition to having to blast a channel hundreds of feet deep, much of it solid rock, the engineers were constantly checked by thousands of tons of hillside sliding into the canal and causing flooding. The excavation in this section alone amounted to the removal of 230,000,000 cubic yards of spoil.

We now steamed into the last system of locks before finally entering Panama City Bay under Thatcher Bridge, now called the Bridge of the Americas, then out into the Pacific Ocean turning north-west to track 100 miles off the coasts of Costa Rica, Nicaragua, El Salvador and Guatemala respectively. During the next few days of steaming up the South American coast-line, cricket matches were again in full swing. Possibly because of my uneventful play, I had been delegated to official match scorer, a task that for some unknown reason warranted an extra pint of beer at the end of each match!!

November 29th – Mexico 8.00 am.

We steamed into Acapulco Bay, which must be one of the finest natural harbours in the world. The weather was perfect, even at this time of day the air temperature was 83 degrees F, 28 degrees C with a North-west wind force 2. I dread to think what the weather is like at this moment back in fog shrouded Britain. Once anchor was cast passengers were ferried ashore by tender. 'Acapulco' the very name conjures up a dream world, few areas on earth can match. The natural grandeur of Acapulco's beaches, the blue of its skies and waters, the wonderful climate plus of course the Acapulco Princess which claims to be the most beautiful hotel in the world. A playground for the rich, the famous and the villainous. But that is the icing on the cake, vast numbers of Mexicans are poor, some desperately so like the riffraff that met us as soon as we stepped ashore. Unwashed individuals, long haired teenagers and young mothers with babies swarmed round us like vultures pressing us to buy straw hats, trinkets, souvenirs and catchpenny ornaments. Pushing our way through the throng whilst showing no desire to buy only caused the pedlars to get more and more desperate, dropping their asking price by the second, pleading to our better nature. Any method to sell and obtain those precious American dollars or English pounds. In the end one is almost forced to purchase some unwanted item, but surrender solves nothing. Others are quick to notice that you are a soft touch and swarm round you, however once clear of the harbour we took tour "B". Safe from the vultures at last, an air conditioned coach whisked us away through the city and beyond to witness the 'must' in Acapulco. The death defying cliff divers who after offering prayers to the gods for their safety dive off a rock 136 feet above the waves out and down into an inlet which is only 17 feet wide, timing their dive to hit the water as the next wave comes in, even then they have only 9 or 10 feet of water depth. The diver then swims to the beach, climbs a long flight of steps and hopefully makes a monetary collection. I could think of easier and much safer ways of making a living! After just one very interesting day spent in Acapulco we sailed at 6 pm out into the Gulf of California. The next morning I spent some time on the bridge with the officer of the watch. These days so much of the navigational work on board ship is computerised, radar pin points the position of any other vessel in the vicinity, the course is set every 15 minutes and the depth of water recorded in fathoms by echo sounder. It was indeed a surprise to me how the depth varied, giving one an image of the underwater hills, mountains and deep valleys of the Pacific. Full speed ahead making 24.6 knots, our next port of call :- Los Angeles.

Los Angeles, America's third largest city and surrounded by some of the richest farming land in the States. We could not expect to see much of the city in just one brief visit but I loved the place and especially the climate and although I didn't know it then Ruth and I were destined to return in a few years time to spend a holiday with my eldest son Michael and his family who at the time was working in the city, but that is another chapter.

December 1st – Sailing off the coast of California en route for San Francisco.

During the night we ran into the teeth of a force 7 gale, waves crashed over promenade deck, luckily the storm this time was short lived and we soon passed into calmer waters. With the dawn the wind abated, the pelting rain ceased and out came the sun once more. This time neither Ruth or I had been sea-sick- at last we could call ourselves sailors!

December 3rd- off San Francisco

Although Sir Francis Drake sailed to within 30 miles of San Francisco in 1579 the peninsula remained undiscovered for nearly 200 years. It now lays claim to being one of the most beautiful cities in the world. Golden Gate Bridge, 8 miles long linking San Francisco to Oakland on the other side is one of the longest suspension bridges in the world over navigable waters. We passed under the bridge at 7 pm and docked two hours later. Do they ever sleep in San Francisco? It was past midnight when we took a coach tour of the city and the streets were packed with revellers whose thoughts seemed far from sleep. I am told that there are nearly 3,000 restaurants in the whole place and they all seemed packed out! We were driven over the Bay Bridge to Bay City and back over the Golden Gate Bridge to end up in Chinatown which boasts the largest Chinese community outside Asia, larger than the one in New York. Towards dawn we were back to our bunks on the Canberra to try and snatch a few hours sleep.

December 4th
Today Canberra was taking on board essential supplies amongst other things, fresh water, fuel oil and a vast assortment of food for the next leg of our journey. Destination, the volcanic Hawaiian Islands, 2000 miles from the nearest land out in the vast Pacific Ocean. Whilst this preparation was taking place we had another interesting day ashore. We simply had to "do" Fisherman's Wharf- the headquarters of the picturesque fishing fleet which daily from October to August heads out through the Golden Gate for crabs and deep-sea fish. The place is a mecca for tourists and buskers perform here in droves. In the afternoon, for us another excursion this time the Muir Wood. Our route lead us through the Rainbow Tunnel up into the surrounding hills until we reached the coast redwood trees reputed to be the tallest living things on earth. These immense trees are believed to be upwards of 2000 years old and some standing 300 feet above the ground, the tallest of all being the Founder's Tree on Highway 101, towards Oregon, 364 feet tall.

The Redwood's great size and long life are attributed to their high resistance to fires, insects and fungi. Hence the lack of birds in the forest. I found that one of the most noticeable things about San Francisco is the steepness of many of its streets a feature which was responsible I was told for the development of the original cable cars. In our short visit to this American city we sure managed to do a lot of sightseeing.

December 5th

Canberra set course for Hawaii sailing from San Francisco on a west/south westerly transit of the North Pacific Ocean. For days we steamed on and on, not even a glimpse of land, not another boat to be seen, the only sign of life, some flying fish that seemed attracted to the ship and followed us for hours. Day after day the sun shone out of a cloudless sky. The clear blue waters were as still as a millpond with not so much as a breath of wind. If we had been relying on sails we would have been becalmed but for us privileged individuals there was always the reassurance of 85,000 shaft horse power down in the bowels of the ship and a crew of 805!

The eight islands of Hawaii, of which seven are inhabited cover an area of 6,400 square miles- by English comparison, slightly larger than Yorkshire. Honolulu is on the island of Ohau (pronounced O-HA-OO) capital city of America's 50th state. What wonderful memories Ruth and I have of our visit to Ohau and the nearby island of Hula Hula. We swam in the warm waters, sunbathed on the famous Waikiki beach, strolled through plantations of bananas, pineapples and sugar cane and always got such a warm welcome from the islanders. One must not forget of course that these islands haven't always been so peaceful. On a coach tour we visited the Punchbowl National Memorial Cemetery an extinct volcanic crater where 26,000 American Service men are buried or have their names recorded. A sad reminder of the terrible period of the 2nd world war.

Certificate from King Neptune

December 10th

We sailed at midnight on the high tide, our destination Suva capital and chief port of the Fiji Islands. For days we sailed south-west across the vast Pacific Ocean. Days which were pleasantly passed playing deck tennis, deck cricket, quoits or just lazing on the sun deck eating 'free' ice-cream. It's easy to forget they had all been paid for before leaving home! In the cool of the evening we enjoyed the latest cooking delights of the chef washed down by the very best wine followed by either a visit to the cinema, a variety show, or just danced the night away. What a life of luxury? Bully for some!

December 14th

Today we crossed the equator. King Neptune- the Roman god of the sea-and his aquatic court had been invited aboard to ask his permission to cross his domain. All in good fun of course. So tonight there was to be a great party with plenty of merry making. Much homage is made to King Neptune on crossing the equator on a pleasure cruise.

December 14th

For us the day that never was. Clocks were advanced 24 hours due to the fact that we had crossed the international date line. If we really had been attempting to circumnavigate the world in eighty days I would have to take in the fact that at this point in time I had lost a day travelling westwards round the world! But a wager of £20,000 did not lay in abeyance.

December 18th

We rose early to see the sun rise at 5.25 am before entering the harbour at Suva. We were given a ceremonious welcome by the men of the Royal Military Band in their colourful uniforms. On going ashore we were given a fabulous welcome by the natives who seemed so easy going and friendly. There was no mad rush to sell useless trash or take the tourist pounds and dollars at all cost. After getting used to walking on dry land again after many days at sea we took a tour of the city in a windowless bus and then out to Orchid Island by way of a road bridge that connect the two islands.

This was followed by a leisurely stroll around the vegetable market and then after lunch we took another boat trip, this time by a glass bottom cruiser across Suva Harbour to Nukulau Island which is inside the Great Barrier Reef. Slowly cruising over parts of the Reef one gets a fantastic insight into one of natures wonderland. Swarms of colourful fish swimming amongst the coral forest, a sight never to be forgotten and to me one of the highlights of our travels. Coming ashore on a gently sloping sandy beach lapped by a blue Pacific ocean we were greeted by crowds of native children who sang and danced and hung garlands around our necks of sweet smelling "Salu Salus." Further up the shore in the shade of coconut trees the Fijian warriors performed the Meki-Wesi spear dance, a frightening experience if it had been for real. Finally we all sat on the ground in their thatched communal house and partook of South Sea Islands dishes and drank a very potent drink made from coconuts. Of course the whole show is put on for the tourist benefit! I'm sure the Fijiano are the most friendly people on earth.

We got under way from Suva on the 6.00 am high tide, destination New Zealand. Three days later we sailed into Auckland Harbour to a tremendous welcome. Small boats came out to meet us, crowds of people lined the quay, cheering, singing, waving flags all adding to the confusion as the Royal Scots Pipe Band struck up a rousing march. Anxiously I scanned the crowd gathered on the quay side seeking my friends whom I hadn't seen for years. As the Canberra crept closer I picked them out. Sally Juby, her daughter Debbie and young son Marcus waiting to welcome Ruth and me to New Zealand after a trip of six weeks duration and a distance of 15,000 miles. Eventually the time came to leave the ship and say our good-byes to members of the crew whom we had befriended. I walked down the gangplank, solid land once again, my legs were unsteady and I am sure the ground moved!

At this point I must relate the saga of the rocking chair. Our friends, the Juby family on hearing of our proposed journey to New Zealand by boat asked Ruth and me to do them a good turn. Could we bring grandma's rocking chair with us? Now it transpired that in her will Grandma Juby had left Sally an antique rocking chair. Normally this could only be sent over from England at considerable expense but seeing that we were travelling by boat we were allowed to transport a considerably amount of luggage free of charge. Enquiries at the P & O office back in England confirmed that it could travel with us but that I would have to crate it and deliver to the dock in Southampton three days before we were due to sail. Whereupon back at the farm I set to work making a wooden crate. I soon released that to construct a wooden crate large enough to accommodate a fair size rocking chair was no easy task. Slowly the crate took shape but with the chair inside there was lots of empty space all around it, so the only thing to do to prevent it rattling around like a pea in a drum was to pack it out with clothes, blankets and any odds and ends I could find. Unnecessary items all of which they had plenty of in New Zealand. Now the only thing left to do to was to take the crated chair to the docks. It wouldn't go in my car and I didn't want to drive 100 mile return journey with my cattle wagon. My sister had a shooting brake and she owed me a favour. "Yes" she would loan it to me for the day, it seemed like a problem solved. Arriving at dock number 9, I took the car ignition key to open the rear door. The key didn't fit, my sister had the correct key and she was fifty miles away. The rear door could be opened from inside but with the crate completely filling the space there was just no way to open the door. Eventually the A.A were called and they solved the problem by smashing the glass window with an axe. Ha well, I told myself, "not my car". When later I returned my sister's car I wasn't very popular for a while! The crated rocking chair was finally checked in and left at dock number 9, where in due course it disappeared into the holds of the Canberra. We didn't see it again until it was swung ashore in a rope sling at Auckland docks. Grandma's antique rocking chair had arrived. When it finally got to the Juby's farmhouse there where drinks all round when the chair and it's packing was safely uncrated.

Our friends David Juby, his wife, Sally and their six children live on a small hill-top homestead over-looking the country town of Thames. David is a veterinary surgeon with a practice in town. Besides attending to the health of a wide range of small animals his practice covered an area about the size of Berkshire and Wiltshire combined. Ruth and I stayed with the Jubys for some weeks. This gave us a great opportunity to visit stock farms with David and talk to the farmers regarding their everyday problems which I quickly discovered were similar to our own back home. The talk at that time was the weather, would it hold fine? It was nearly Christmas, hay-making time down under. David who was a part-time farmer as well as a vet, had mowed and twice turned his grass and was anxious to get it baled before the 25th. The local contractor turned up on time and in ideal weather baled a heavy crop into handy conventional bales. I soon got stuck into the job of clearing the field, pitching the bales onto the tractor drawn trailer and stacking them in the barn. This job was right up my street. I'd show these New Zealanders how to move bales! Trouble was I'd been cruising the world for the last six weeks, lounging in deck chairs soaking up the sun, living a life of luxury on all the finest foods. Of late, unaccustomed to a bit of hard physical work, I caught the sun working without a shirt on, I got blisters on my hands, and I had done my back in! I didn't get much sympathy from Ruth!

Christmas Eve

David said to me "If your back is better, would you like to come with me to get the Christmas dinner?"

"Yes, I would like to, where are we going, to the butcher in town?" I asked innocently.

"Course not" he replied with a laugh. "We are going to the bush to shoot a turkey or two."

Now that is not as easy as it sounds. Bush turkeys are big birds and it would be difficult to miss one if the hunter is only half a shot, especially as you shot them on the ground. But the problem is to get in range, they are wild and very crafty. The cock-bird can see a hunter coming a mile off and as soon as it senses danger it makes a heck of a racket. When we eventually reached turkey country David concealed himself in dense shrub and I was dispatched in a wide circle to get behind our quarry with instructions to drive the birds towards the waiting gun. If I could get them within range, David knew he would only get one chance. A left and right, after that they would be gone in a half fly, half run, escaping at high speed. Our hunt was successful, two birds for the pot, but I can tell you there is not much meat on a wild turkey. Give me one of Bernard Matthew's any day! And another thing, something seemed amiss with the fact that we ate our Christmas fare sitting in the garden trying to get some shade under the table canopy from the blazing midday sun. There is something more Christmassy sitting in front of a blazing log fire with snow flakes gently falling outside.

In the days that followed Ruth and I spent many interesting hours accompanying David on his veterinary rounds. On one occasion when David and the farmer were attending to a difficult calving case Ruth and I took over the milking of two hundred dairy cows and whilst on another call we helped to worm 500 sheep before lunch! Although I'd be the first to admit, it wasn't all work. David and Sally took two days off from the daily grind taking us into the rain forest to discover the Devoich Kauri Tree, the third largest Kauri on the Coromandel Peninsular. By any yardstick the Kauri is a monarch amongst trees. After a few hours trek through what is truly a beautiful area of trees, delicate ferns, parasite plants, clinging creepers and hosts of colourful birds there it was, this gigantic tree. Like a solid wall blocking the path. By far the biggest tree in girth I had ever seen. It towered way above all the other trees in the forest with a girth of 10.54 metres and a volume of 101 cubic metres. Historic note:- this tree was first sighted in 1900 by Nick Yates and for some reason was then lost to the civilised world until an expedition rediscovered it in 1966. Not so long ago. Such is the denseness of the Waipoua Forest that giants such as this maybe passed quite close without seeing them.

It was on our return journey from our visit to the Kauri Tree that a possible disaster was narrowly adverted. The 'girls' namely Sally and Ruth stepped off the main trail to attend to the call of nature. David and I continued to slowly follow the path if one could call it that. On returning to the trail the ladies turned left instead of right making their way back the way we had just come. We dawdled on but all the time we were getting further and further away from each other. Finally we realised our partners were missing. Although calling out at the top of our voices we could get no reply. We were to learn later that when they failed to catch us up they had only walked faster and faster getting further and further away from us. It was only when they got back to the giant tree that they realised what had happened. It was all of two hours before we met up again and we still had the long hike back to base.

Early in the New Year we sadly took leave of the Juby family. Heading south we were driven by Mary Hayes, a friend whom Ruth had helped in the past when she had been in difficulties with her marriage. She took us to visit her parents Bill and Mary Mayo who farmed at Marton in the vicinity of Mount Egmont. That beautiful mountain with it's perpetual snow cap. After two days of rest from our travels the Mayo's took Ruth and me on a tour of the area in their battered Landrover. Some of the places we visited were Wanganui, Palmerston North, Mackenze Rose Garden and another interesting experience was to go to Bill's son's farm through the Whakangaramanga Valley (which by the way means narrow hidden stream in Maori) We followed a gravel track deep into the bush for a distance of 28 miles until the farm was reached. This reclaimed hill land supports some 800 merino ewes kept mainly for their wool. What an isolated place to live. Still he had no neighbours to quarrel with!

The Cook Strait between North and South Island is notoriously rough so we took a short plane flight to Nelson on

South Island. I didn't know a soul in Nelson, the hotels were all full due to the fact that there was some annual festival on at the time and we couldn't find a B & B. Luck was on my side as always. I found a caravan park and the proprietor put us up for the night in a vacant mobile home. In fact it turned out to be quite comfortable.

Our itinerary, if one could call it that, was to visit Wilfred and Joan Begg who with their married son Russel farm at Totara Flat on the West coast. Over the years I had kept in touch by letter ever since my second son Tony had worked on their farm in 1971 as a middle year student in agriculture. Rising early after a good nights sleep I had paid my dues and we got on our way. We hadn't had any breakfast except for two biscuits and a cup of tea without sugar or milk. Nelson was unduly quiet as we walked down the main street, making for the bus station where we just managed to catch the only bus of the day bound for Greymouth. The second class road winds through beautiful pine covered hills, skirts the coast here and there, a coast of sandy beaches and isolated coves with little sign of habitation. When we did pass a few houses the driver slowed down and tossed out the mail and daily papers.

Occasionally we stopped to pick up another passenger or set one off, but it seemed that only the two of us were going right through. We made a courtesy stop at Pancake Rocks and it was but a few miles later that on rounding a sharp bend in mountainous country the bus could go no further. The road ahead was completely blocked by a huge landslide following the recent heavy rains in the area. The driver of the bus walked back a couple of miles to a telephone. Eventually with the aid of a bulldozer and explosives the road was cleared, but we were three hours late arriving at Greymouth. A phone call to Wilfred did get us to Totara Flat in due course. Joan a motherly soul, bless her, had prepared a first class meal of roast beef and three veg followed by apple pie and cream. We hadn't had any breakfast and had eaten little all day, we sure tucked into that feast. I think her first impression of these English guests was that we were going to be an expensive couple to keep!

Totara Flat: It is flat, very flat. Excellent grazing country. Arguably some of the best farmland in New Zealand.

Wilfred and Russel fattened a 1,000 cattle a year and if that wasn't enough they ran 600 breeding ewes. They were mustering and shearing sheep at the time of our visit. A batch of ewes had that day been rounded up to be kept undercover overnight ready for an early start on shearing. The procedure was for Russel and his father to pull the ewes out and push them through for the four contract shearers, and two girls were kept busy tying the fleeces. Ruth helped out in the farmhouse preparing meals for everybody, and my job? Take the workers their smoke-o (Eleven's in England) I felt a pang of sympathy for the four men shearing. It must take some sticking hour after hour day after day stripped to the waist, sweat pouring off their brow, and all for 60 cents a time. No wonder Aussies and New Zealanders like their beer!

January 12 1983
7.30 am we took leave of our new found friends, Wilfred drove us to Stillwater station. Lugging our two bulging suitcases mostly filled with unsuitable clothes and souvenirs acquired on our travels which we didn't really need, we caught a two coached diesel train bound for Christchurch on the eastern coast of South Island. This proved to be a very interesting and scenic journey. First the rails pass through range after range of mountains then through a five mile tunnel, followed by a brief stop at Otira after which we negotiate Arthur's Pass. I counted 17 railway tunnels on this spectacular mountain section until dropping down to the vast Canterbury Plain. Sheep, I've never seen so many- now I know where New Zealand lamb comes from!!

Christchurch railway station. Awaiting us was Martine Juby, Sally and David's eldest daughter who had an apartment in the city. She was expecting us of course. How nice to have friends spread all over the world. We were taken on a guided tour of the city before enjoying a meal which Martine had prepared for us. Everyone is so kind. After a restful nights sleep we had to say our good-byes before catching a plane which was to take us to North Island. This time to Napier. At the airport we were met by Bill and June Drummond, farming folk who had befriended my youngest son Fred when he had come to New Zealand to work. Bill, semi retired has a lovely home situated on just 30 acres of hilltop land overlooking beautiful Hawkes Bay. They also own a holiday cottage on the shore of lake Taupo some 80 miles inland and right bang in the middle of North Island. Bill and June seemed delighted to play host to farming folk from England and couldn't do enough for us. One of our trips was to their property in the hills now farmed by his son. I found this very interesting as apart from untold numbers of sheep the son also specialised in farming deer. Something new to me. Selling most of the young hinds at two years old as breeding animals for which at the time there appeared to be an excellent market.

Another great day out was when Bill took Ruth and me to Stortford Lodge Sheep Fair. This was something extra special for me to get amongst the hard-nut farming fraternity especially since Bill knew many of the old-timers. 25,076 breeding ewes were penned that day in an open field reminiscent of East Ilsley's sheep fair of the 1930's back in Berkshire, or the big Wilton sheep fair of today. The big difference was that they were being auctioned in bunches of 200/400 at one go, at prices between 5 to 20 dollars per ewe. A fraction of our prices for the same class of stock back home. Four auctioneers were selling alternatively, moving from pen to pen and assisted by staff whose job was to mouth a sample of each group of ewes and shouting out to prospective buyers the condition of the animals teeth. Broken

The world's first sunrise everyday. Napier N.Z.

mouth ewes – those with few or no teeth because of age- made considerably less money due to the fact that they cannot eat enough grass to support lambs as well as themselves and were coming to the end of their natural breeding lives. Luckily we found time to spend a week at the Drummond's cottage adjacent to Lake Taupo, and whilst there we did managed to get in a few days fishing. The trout caught on this lake are reputed to be amongst the biggest in the world, and when barbecued make marvellous eating.

We had many more adventures in this part of the world, too many to relate in this book but one I should mention was to take a tractor and trailer ride seven miles along Hawkes Bay beach to Cape Kidnappers which can only be attempted while the tide is out. There to view in close up what is claimed to be the only mainland Gannet Colony in the world. I must say it is quite a sight to see 2000 pairs of birds nesting on this rocky

Gannets on Cape Kidnappers

promontory and what a racket they kick up.

When a shoal of fish came in close we had an excellent view of these magnificent birds in action, diving into the sea at speeds of up to 60 miles an hour scooping up a fish and then return to regurgitate a partly digested meal for its one solitary chick. By taking my life into my hands I climbed up to the top of some high cliffs and obtained my best photo to date. A close up picture of a pair of Gannets. And my camera hasn't got a telephoto lens!

Next stop Rotorua:
I guess in time one gets used to the heat, boiling mud, geysers recurring at regular intervals and the continuous smell of sulphur but it the last place on earth I should choose to live. Yet that it is just what my friends Jeanne and Bart Long choose to

do. Years ago Bart was a police sergeant in Newbury and for a time would come out to Mousefield Farm to shoot pigeons in his off duty periods. He retired a young 45 year old, sold his house and moved to Rotorua of all places. We just had to call and stay for a few days. It goes without saying that they were more than pleased to see us, they get few visitors from England. The highlight of our visit was to enjoy an outdoor supper cooked by means of trapping super heated steam escaping from vents in the rocks. After a marvellous meal of local fish, wild boar and all the trimmings the Moari residents performed their nerve racking war dance. With almost naked bodies bedecked with paint, waving spears and charging menacingly to within feet of the audience, extending their tongues, eyes rolling and pulling the most horrible faces. Something similar to the All Blacks demonstrations given before each rugger match as seen on T.V. but much more intimidating when face to face with the real thing.

On old shooting partner of mine Gordon Vosper now sadly departed had farming relatives living at Matamata. Before we left England, on hearing of my proposed visit to New Zealand had said to me "Now you will be sure to call and see Maurice and Beth Vosper whilst you are over there won't you?"

"If we get within a 100 miles I will call." I promised him, lightly dismissing the difficulties of travelling such distances when one is in a strange country and without wheeled transport. Now I know there are trains and buses but dragging two big suitcases and a couple of overnight bags can get you down a bit after a while. However, we had promised to return to our friends the Jubys before leaving for home. Apparently they had planned a holiday to the coast which was to include Ruth and me. On studying the map I realised that Matamata was somewhere between Rotorua and Thames. The opportunity to visit yet another dairy unit was too great to miss.

Maurice Vosper makes an hard-earned living milking 104

pedigree jersey cows on 160 acres. He and his loyal wife make an excellent job of it. They gave us a very warm welcome and we spent a few very pleasant days relaxing in this lovely part of the country. Of course dairy farming looks easy when the grass grows for eleven months of the year and the cows never have to be housed in the winter. Just turn them out into the fields on wonderful wild white clover pastures with its claim to be the richest and most heavily stocked dairy pasture in the world. It is also horse racing country but that's another story.

Maurice and Beth kindly drove us in their car back to the Jubys. On arrival almost the whole family were there to welcome Ruth and me back "home" again. David, Sally, Debbie, Nigel, Marcus, and their golden labrador plus two horses, an incalf Jersey cross Friesian heifer, twenty ewes and lambs, 70 goats and an assortment of hens, bantams and angora rabbits with a hive or two of bees thrown in where all there to welcome us back from our travels. It really felt great to be back with such warm hearted friends again.

"We are all going on holiday and you two are coming with us won't that be lovely?" The whole family chorused.

Pauanui: Spells sun, sand and the beautiful warm Pacific. One of New Zealand's finest beaches. We spent leisurely days swimming, cresting the waves on surfboards or just soaking up the sun. We even found time to get in some fishing taking out a hired boat to fish off Shoe Island. David, Marcus, Ruth and I concentrated on catching blue fish, a colourful inhabitant of waters north of East Cape. They are easily identified by their violet-blue colour with brilliant yellow spots. They are a good challenge to the fisherman being powerful fighters and can reach up to 30 inches in length and what's more they are excellent barbecued. According to my notes on our best day we caught 14 fish, Ruth caught 12 of them so that doesn't speak well of her companions' skill with the rod and line!

The time had come for us to complete our circumnavigation

of the globe. We flew out of Auckland airport on a Boeing 747, touched down briefly at Perth then again to refuel in Singapore before arriving home to a snow covered England on the 2nd February. What a contrast to an Australasian Summer!

Austria and the World of Poppen

As the summer of 1992 approached its close, August 27th in this pleasant rural area of the Thames Valley was just another wet day, yet no wetter than the string of wet and windy days that this month had thrown at English farmers and the once a year holiday maker heading for the coast. Ruth and I were off to the sun, at least we were hoping so, to Austria and "The World of Poppen". Friedrich and Jutta Poppen had, in previous years, stayed bed and breakfast at Mousefield Farm then, as friendship developed, as our guests at Stable Cottage, our second home across the valley.

We had gratefully accepted their kind invitation to visit them and in so doing they could return our hospitality. My step daughter Sue, always so kind and willing, drove Ruth and me to Reading railway station to catch the 1.33 pm train to Gatwick. Farewells said, a last wave and we were on our travels once again. It is a pleasant journey through the rolling Berkshire and Surrey countryside, cattle and sheep graze green pastures, tractors plough the stubble of harvested crops, but the remaining arable fields of wheat and spring barley looked a sorry sight, battered, twisted and rain washed. Whatever has happened to the "greenhouse" effect of the previous couple of years when the harvest was dry and safe in store by mid August?

We had tickets to fly Britannia Airways flight BY0538 leaving at 3.30 pm for Salzburg, in fact we were not airborne until 3.45 pm, yet after an uneventful flight our Captain touched down safely on time. Salzburg, the capital of the province of the same name, lies on the northern slopes of the Alps, almost at the centre of Austria. Its world wide reputation is due, primarily to its incomparable natural setting, also its fine architecture and the fact that W A Mozart was born there in 1756. One of the first things I noticed on alighting from the plane were the red and white flags of Austria flying everywhere, did they know we were coming, I wonder?

As expected our friends were awaiting us in the arrival lounge, greetings exchanged we were whisked away in their gleaming white Mercedes on a round about route to Bad Aussee and our first glimpse of the scenic Austrian countryside with its lakes, mountains, rivers and alpine meadows. My first impression was a feeling of unlimited space and a desire to explore further. Friedrich suggested that, if we would like a meal, we should go to a restaurant before going on to their home. This would allow us to arrive at their "dirty little house" after dark. This description of their abode was, of course, far from the truth, in reality it turned out to be even more luxurious than I had imagined.

Built on rising ground in a beautiful alpine valley where cattle graze lush green pastures, roe deer come out to feed at dusk and traditional Austrian houses dot the countryside. The whole surrounded by snow capped mountains and in the far distance, through a break in the peaks, can be seen the Dachstein at a height of 3004 metres it is the highest mountain in the Dachsteinruppe range. From our view point in the valley the sun reflects varying shades of grey and white off the glazier face. A world of eternal snow and ice.

Our friend's home in the mountains of Austria

Our friends' house is well designed and tastefully furnished, everything planned for comfort and to cope with the extremes of weather that summer and winter bring in this part of the world. Friedrich's hunting trophies are displayed everywhere and he takes great pleasure in relating in detail the location and demise of each and everyone. Yet they are unobtrusive and add character to this interesting house. The home of a man who has done so much for his country.

Ruth and I were escorted to the guest bedroom, it was spacious with ample room for the king-size four poster bed, the huge leather settee and the fitted wardrobes. A dense deep pile, mauve coloured carpet adds more luxury and cushioned my feet as I walked across the room, almost reverently, to place our cases on the rack provided.

Double glazed glass doors lead out to a private flower decked balcony and the mountains seemed so close across the meadow that you felt you could lean over and pick fir cones from the tree tops. It goes without saying that we had an en-suite bathroom with plush carpets, floor to ceiling tiles and a bath large enough to drown in if you couldn't swim!

The next morning, breakfast, continental style, was taken outside on the patio. The weather was pleasantly warm and the summer sun shone out of a cloudless sky. Despite the slight language barrier conversation flowed, we had so much news to catch up on since our last meeting earlier in the year. On this, our first full day in Austria, our hosts suggested a swim! Not in the nearby town leisure centre, but in a mountain trapped lake. This necessitated a stiff two kilometre walk, climbing all the way to a height of 1000 metres above sea level, although it must be stated that our starting point was set at 650 metres. If one wasn't feeling energetic it was possible to drive a motor vehicle to this popular spot and this was apparently how the many other sunbathers and swimmers had made the journey. The lake swarmed with fish, its dark green water unpolluted. I was pleasantly surprised how warm the water was and we thoroughly enjoyed a refreshing swim before making for the lakeside cafe to slake our thirst in a half litre of Kaiser Bier.

The whole of this money making sideline was a diversification project run by the farmer who owns the lake and surrounding land. I had the opportunity to chat with him, Friedrich acting as interpreter. On his small holding he kept ten or twelve cows, milking them by hand and sending the milk off each day to the local creamery. Naturally he charged an entry fee to his lake, and served refreshments at the cafe his wife and himself acting as waiters. It seemed an idyllic way to make a living, but no doubt a very different story prevails in the winter months, when the whole area is under two metres of snow, with access only possible by ski or helicopter. The grass always looks greener on the other side of the fence, except perhaps when covered by snow!!

That evening our hosts drove us through the little town of Bad Aussee to dine at the See villa restaurant. Set on a rise of high ground above a beautiful lake, it was all so romantic. The full moon seemed suspended in space between two mountain peaks, shining so bright it cast shadows on the ground, whilst beyond the waters edge myriads of lights twinkled from the lakeside houses. From the extensive menu I chose Zander filet and Ruth the Kalbsleber. In all, the total bill for four came to 1001 schillings plus service charge of 5%, which included an early beer and two bottles of Rutlander Pinot Gris 1990. Very reasonable at just over fifty pounds in English money.

The next day was a Saturday, not that the day makes much difference when you are on holiday. We rose late from the comfort of our four-poster to be greeted by another beautiful morning. Ruth returned from the bathroom to find me out on the balcony, bewitched by the beauty of our surroundings. "If you ever write about all this on our return I don't suppose you will know how to describe it"? she murmured, thoughtfully trying not to disturb my concentration. "I'm inclined to agree with you my dear, my vocabulary is much too limited" I replied.

Today was to prove a lazy one, after a protracted breakfast we wrote postcards to family and friends, read a little, talked a lot. On the agenda was the possibility of Friedrich and Jutta coming to England, in the May or July of 1993, to shoot roebuck on my small country estate. We were getting overrun with deer and the need to reduce their numbers was becoming a matter of urgency. If this had to be done I would wish no better marksman than Friedrich Poppen. The certainty of a bullet through the heart brings humane and instant death to surplus roebuck, it also ensures my freezer will contain a goodly supply of venison the following winter.

August 30th, a severe thunderstorm had raged through most of the night. Heavy rain pelted the double glazed windows and rattled on the slate roof, whilst lightening lit up the night sky and the thunder boomed and echoed around nearby mountain peaks making sleep hard to come by. Breakfast outside on the patio was out of the question, the air was damp and the overnight rain had left a nip in the air, hence our first meal of the day was eaten around the solid oak dining table in the warmth of the house. Fine bread, various pate, finely sliced meat, numerous cheeses and sundry jams. Percolated coffee and the finest fresh fruits completed the spread. Truly a continental breakfast to be remembered. After such a meal it was 11.00 am before we made a move, when we did it was to drive by car some 20 kilometres to the interesting town of Altausee. After a saunter round the shops, many of which were rather quaint we continued to the nearby lake. The clear unpolluted water consisting of snow melt and rain which runs off the surrounding mountains that soar upwards on three sides to almost encircle this idyllic spot. The lake was very deep, 160 metres in places and the trees pressed down the mountain slopes right to the very edge, yet it was possible to walk the whole way round following a well-maintained path, a hike of seven and half kilometres (5 miles). Walking at a leisurely pace we did it in two hours. This time included a short stop in a secluded bay where we were tempted to remove shoes and socks and dip our feet in the water. There was another delay when we were entertained by a duck and her four well-grown ducklings. The mother swam around with watchful eyes whilst her charges dived deep to feed amongst huge rocks, which littered the bottom of the lake in this area. Standing high above the clear water we got an excellent view of these little creatures, highly adapted to their environment and capable of staying under water for long periods. That evening we dined at the lakeside restaurant and for some unknown reason I chose roast duck from the menu. The meal was well prepared and presented but as I delved into my portion the thought crossed my mind that the drake had

On the way up the Loser

been missing from the little family group on the lake earlier in the day !

The forecast for August 31st was for a continuation of the anticyclone, a spiral flow of air out from an area of high atmospheric pressure, which of course would herald more sunshine but cooler than of late. What better day to climb the "Loser," the highest mountain in the immediate district. It was no big deal really, one can drive by car two thirds of the way, albeit a tortuous route with severe gradients and numerous hairpin bends. Doing just that we eventually reached the ski resort set on a plateau high on the mountain side, at fifteen hundred metres. After parking the car we donned hiking gear before setting off up the marked trail which leads to the summit, a two hour climb in good conditions. For the first part the path snakes upwards, just a moderate climb until it traverses a ridge,

84

and there below was an enchanting small lake, unseen from the lower slopes, which makes its discovery all the more of a surprise. We got another surprise too, from our view point we looked down on nude bathers!! Three pretty girls enjoying the solitude of this isolated spot, the white of their bare buttocks contrasted vividly against the rest of their bronze lithe bodies as they dived off a rock into the crystal clear water, surfaced and waved cheekily to their audience. Feeling rather guilty at our intrusion into their privacy we moved swiftly on our way. As we climbed higher the route became rocky and more difficult. It was at this stage that Friedrich decided to quit. He was finding the altitude caused his heart to race, also Jutta dropped out because she was not wearing the correct footwear. Having got so far, and due to the fact that Ruth and I may not pass this way again, we pressed on. The higher we got the more difficult the route became, but on the more dangerous sections a steel wire is held to the rock face by piton. These guides were a great help to hold onto as we traversed the mountain's south-west face. After passing through a huge fissure we came to the "Window" a natural rock formation, the size of a small house. Set on the crest of a ridge it gave a magnificent view into the next valley. To look down from the "Window" is quite a frightening experience, there was no warning notice, no guard rail, just a huge lump of granite, like a giant mint with a hole in it, balancing on the edge, the precipice falling almost sheer to the valley one thousand metres below. From this point the going became easier and a more gentle route leads upwards to the top, but alas like most mountains the last peak was tantalisingly hiding yet another one higher still. Finally weary and rather breathless we stood on the summit of the Loser. At eighteen hundred and thirty eight metres, it is almost twice the height, above sea level, as Mount Snowdon. The journey down took much less time but even so was far from easy. Our friends were still patiently waiting on the lower slopes and expressed their

The mountain window on the Loser

surprise that someone who'd had major heart surgery should have reached the summit of the Loser!

September 1st, during the night much rain had fallen with very heavy snow on the mountain peaks. It was fortunate that we climbed the Loser yesterday for the ill equipped and inexperienced, such as Ruth and me it would have been out of the question a day later. Instead we chose to spend our time in Bad Ischl, an old imperial town and health resort. A really charming city, built astride the river Traun, rather different in many ways from other spas. Visiting a town to shop is not one of my favourite pastimes, however shopping in Ischl I found to be quite interesting. Folklore, fashions, curios and antique shops abounded and the sales staff were most courteous. Ruth succeeded in buying a skirt, blouse and black leather belt, an acquisition that did much to make a dull weather day brighter, but I must add that I got quite a shock when the manager presented the bill, two thousand five hundred and eighty eight schillings, which seemed a vast sum until a quick mental calculation assured me that in English money the sum represents about £125 !

After the recent heavy rain a fine day was forecast for September 2nd, we had planned to visit Werfenweng, a small rural town just off the A10 autobahn, forty kilometres south east of Salzburg. It was here in the foothills of the mountains that our friends had their second home. The main reason for our visit was the fact that, having put the house on the market, Friedrich had an appointment with the estate agent. Not wishing to intrude in any business conversation we asked to be dropped off at the end of the village. From this point Ruth and I set off across alpine meadows, in which small herds of dairy cows grazed, contentedly, on the short, unfertilised grass. For the next hour or so we climbed steadily into the foothills of nearby mountains. Overhead, steel cables of the ski lift attached at intervals to metal pylons, span the valleys, marching upwards following a wide swath cut through the mountain slope forest, until disappearing from view amongst the solitude of high peaks. Quiet and peaceful at that time of the year, yet a world that would come to life with the arrival of winter snow.

On our return we stopped for a drink at a beer garden to meet Friedrich once more. In the course of conversation he asked "would you like to meet a farmer friend of mine?" "Yes I certainly would" I replied. Subsequently he drove us to the other side of the valley, where he introduced us to Peter and Wetti Rohrmoser, the farmer and his wife. It was to prove an interesting afternoon. A large farm for the area, covering some sixty hectares, all down to grass, except for a small section of hillside. The Austrian farmer informed us that he milked twenty cows and had twenty five followers, beef and dairy replacements. The cows milked by a two unit milking machine and the milk stored in a very tiny, stainless steel mobile bulk tank, mobile so that it could be wheeled to a collecting point further down the valley. What struck me most was the absolute cleanliness of the place. It had been raining, but not a scrap of mud was to be seen, no smelly heaps of dung, no old rubber tyres or black plastic around the yard. Everything in its allotted place.

Invited into the beautiful, three hundred year old farm house it soon became apparent that the cows were not the main source of income. Three stories high with a cellar below, a large modern kitchen, two well laid out dining rooms plus a dozen or so bedrooms. This was bed and breakfast on a grand scale.

Only half an hour from Salzburg, if anyone is interested here you go:-

URLAUB AUF DEM BAUERNHOF — Holidays on a Farm

BALKONZIMMER MIT DUCHE UND W.C — Bedrooms with Bath & W.C.

SONNENTERRASSE LAND SALZBURG
A5453 WERFENWENG Nr 16

Bed and Breakfast for 200 schillings per adult – In English money just £10. Great hospitality, I'd recommend it winter or summer.

Following a late, extended breakfast on September 3rd it was almost midday before setting off on a mystery tour, planned by our generous hosts. We were driven through some of the most scenic landscape in this part of Austria, a circular route which eventually took us through the pleasing village of Grundlsee. This picturesque area with its small farmsteads, antiquated wooden houses and with many of the older folk still dressed in traditional Austrian clothes we got the feeling that apart from the tourists, this remote backwater had changed little in the last century. After parking the car we walked a gravel path, which meanders, through quiet pine forests until eventually reaching a beautiful stretch of clear water. From the banks of this lake white limestone cliffs rose sheer, towering five hundred metres or more blocking out the sun for a large portion of the day. As luck would have it we were just in time to get aboard the next boat for a trip to the far end of the lake.

The wooden boats are of quite an interesting design, seating for twenty eight persons and driven by a small outboard motor, they are constructed rather like a native canoe with a high prow set well clear of the water. Once we got out across the lake the scenery was just fantastic. In several places waterfalls cascaded from high above adding yet more volume to the black, cool water that plunged to great depths. The story goes that Hitler, realising the tide of war was turning against him, ordered that gold, silver and millions in forged foreign notes be placed into steel casks and then dropped for safety into the lake! Apparently some have been recovered, but not all. I rather think, like the Loch Ness monster, it is a gimmick to attract the tourist.

On reaching the far end of the lake our boatman put everyone ashore and from here we had the opportunity to climb steps and stroll through the forest to find "The jewel in the crown" Toplitzee, a tiny land-locked lake inaccessible except by the route we had just come. The sunlight filtered through tall trees exploding silently upon the still waters reflecting many and varied colours. Waterlillies ringed the shore and the first autumn leaves fluttered down to float away in the breeze. We spent some time in this lovely spot in peaceful meditation, but sadly the time came to leave, the last boat would soon be on its way.

That evening we were joined by friends of Friedrich and Jutta and dined at a luxurious restaurant at Grundlsee. Set high above the water it commanded an enchanting position with fine views across the lake. We all enjoyed a very pleasant evening,

On the salt mine train

the music, the wine and the well presented meal, all very romantic. Conversation flowed, in both languages no doubt boosted by liberal quantities of wine, beer and the inevitable Schnapps, the drink so favoured in that part of the world. Unfortunately, like all life's pleasures, time calls the tune, only then did I realise a new day had already dawned.

The weather changed during the night with cold air sweeping down off the mountains, now on the morning of September 4th an icy wind blew and rain battered at the windows, way across the valley the stark summit of the Loser was cloaked in a mantle of new snow. I found it hard to believe that just four days previously we had climbed those treacherous slopes. With such inclement weather our friends suggested a visit to the heart of a mountain would be more appropriate than climbing one. At least we wouldn't get wet and it was immaterial whether the sun came out or not!

"Erlebnis Salzbergwerk" these were the ancient salt mines still being worked in the mountains overlooking the interesting little town of Bad Ischl. Whilst still in operation the mines are also a local tourist attraction. First a ticket was bought at a cost of 100 schillings (£5) and we were allocated ill fitting protective clothing which succeeded in making everyone, both male and female, look like oversized Michelin men. We rode in open carriages pulled by a small but powerful diesel locomotive, right into the centre of the mountain, a distance of over two kilometres. Sitting five or six persons to a truck, one behind the other, we clung nervously to the person in front. The train rattled and shook along uneven rails almost in complete darkness except for a small searchlight on the engine way up ahead. It was very much like riding the ghost train at the local fair! After what seemed an age we emerged into a more brightly lit area, some sort of underground station. Asked to dismount we now discovered that to get to the workings, we had to descend to a lower level and the quickest way to get there was to sit on your backside on a giant wooden slide, lean back, stick your legs out well clear of the sides and with a none too gentle shove from someone behind, you were on your way at an hair-raising, unstoppable pace. The adventure proved to be an unexpected bonus which most people seemed to be enjoying, judging by the exhilarating screams. At the lower level we were in a vast underground cavern with the unsupported rock roof just a couple of metres above our heads and there stood attentively in a circle whilst our guide gave a very detailed explanation of how the salt was mined, extracted and refined. Unfortunately since it was given in German, with my knowledge of the language limited, I was little the wiser at the end of the lecture. However Friedrich gave Ruth and me a translation and from this we gathered that salt has been mined from this mountain for the last three hundred years. The process has been modernised which eliminates much of the hard, dangerous work of earlier times, but it is not a career which I would recommend. Give me the wide open spaces, fresh air and green grass, even if it does rain and blow and the mud sticks to your wellies like glue. Time to go, a blast on a horn vibrates through the honeycomb mountain, our miniature train, the last of the day, is about to leave on the return journey to the outside world. I had no desire to spend the next twenty four hours down a salt mine.

The following day it was time to depart, leaving our friends and beautiful, romantic Austria. On the flight back to England the Captain's voice came over the speaker to announce that despite a strong headwind and a delayed start we would be landing on time. The weather we could expect at Gatwick was 12 degrees C with poor visibility, low cloud level and heavy rain!!

Ah well, what does one expect of an English Summer!

Across the Arctic Circle and Beyond

I had long cherished a desire to visit Norway to cruise up the long Fjords to see for myself the truly magnificent scenery of that long rugged coast line.

Early in January 1987, unbeknown to my wife Ruth, I booked a double berth on a fourteen day cruise on the Canberra. Cruise 706 "To the roof of the world and the Land of the midnight sun." Always a highlight of the Canberra's year, this fjord cruise is truly one of the world's greatest travel experiences, so the organisers claim. In my estimation it is not an exaggeration.

June 18th was departure date. Finally, our cases packed, enough clothes and footwear for a two month trip, let alone a two weeks cruise. Until now our English summer had produced precious little in the way of sunshine, hopefully in those far northern waters, at this time of the year, the sun could be with us twenty four hours a day. In fact I later discovered that perpetual daylight is a mixed blessing, it is not easy to get to sleep, with the sun still high in the sky.

Even though I am supposed to be retired there seemed so many jobs to be done, things to organise before we could finally leave Mousefield in the very capable hands of my three sons and stepdaughter, Sue. My faithful gun dog Tina was granted a last chance to flush a rabbit, which was bowled over smartly by a single shot from my twelve bore shotgun. She retrieved perfectly, this is her life. Back to the farmhouse, "Come on Tina, kennel for you for the next two weeks." As I closed the wire gate, she gazed at me with those sad brown eyes, she seemed to know all the activity and packing of the last few hours meant something different to the usual routine was afoot.

Our deadline for departure from the farm was 3.00 pm. Bound for Southampton we got away thirty minutes late. Sue and grandchildren Catherine, Edward, Ruth and I plus two large suit cases and our hand luggage was somehow squeezed into Sue's Renault Five, 'The little car that thinks big', so the manufacturers rightly claimed.

In forty-five minutes, mostly done at eighty miles per hour, Sue swung into Western Avenue, following the well sign-posted route to Southampton's dock 10. Even whilst still some distance off we heard excited cries from the back seat of "there she is Grandma" as the children picked out Canberra's distinctive twin yellow funnels towering above the cranes and dock side warehouses.

We drove into a large building at berth 106. Our cases were then colour labelled according to which deck our cabin was on. Each and every one subjected to a security check before transfer in huge cord nets, and hoisted aboard by a giant crane, where swarms of dark skin Genoese sailors quickly transported them to the correct cabin. We said our goodbyes, Ruth shed a few tears at the thought of leaving the children, even though it was only for a couple of weeks. Bye Bye, a last turn to wave as we passed through the double doors where our passports were carefully scrutinised, a quick glance and we were waved on with a cheery "Have a good trip".

This was Ruth's and my third cruise on the Canberra, yet

when one gets close to this beautiful ship one tends to gape in awe at its gigantic dimensions. The great white whale its sometimes called. Our footwear clanged loudly on the metal steps of the gangplank, until we emerged at the top on D Deck to be greeted by smiling crew members and the words "Welcome aboard." Everyone was so friendly and cheerful, they greeted us with enthusiasm, like members of a large family returning home after a long absence.

The slightly built Genoese steward, smartly uniformed and wearing white kid gloves, relieved us of our hand luggage turned and lead the way across the thickly carpeted foyer, up the stairs and along the highly polished corridors to cabin C239, our well appointed little room with its bunk beds. Small, yes, but very comfortable. We have found, from past experience, that money is wasted on large stateroom type cabins, after all you spend the minimum of time in your room, there is always such a lot to do and see aboard a pleasure cruiser. Canberra can be a confusing ship to the newcomer, but it becomes easier to find your way around if you bear in mind that you can, in fact, go from one end of the ship to the other on A, B, Promenade, C and D decks. Most of the lounges are either on Promenade or games decks, except the Alice Springs bar which is situated aft on B deck.

June 18th 1987 7.04pm

Canberra slipped her moorings, coloured streamers thrown by departing passengers to friends and relatives waving on the quay side seemed to hold the two groups together. The colourful band of the Dorset Regiment struck a rousing note as they played 'Anchors Away' and the emotional tune "We Are Sailing'. At first the movement of the ship was imperceptible but as the streamers started to break we really were on our way.

Canberra proceeded down Southampton Water to disembark the Pilot off the Nab Tower before entering the Dover Strait in the early hours of Sunday morning.

Ruth and I unpacked our cases before making our way to enjoy a first class dinner in the richly redecorated Atlantic restaurant, before relaxing in the Ocean Room to the music of Bryan Smith and his dance band. We were very lucky that our table companions turned out to be a happy-go-lucky couple, John and Sheila Moore from the Midlands. We were to become good friends for the rest of our cruise, spending most of our evenings together.

By 4.30 am on the Sunday morning we had cleared the Dover Strait and had set a north easterly course through the off-lying oilfields to transcend the North Sea. Sunday morning broke clear and warm, the sun shone through thin high clouds, hazy mists on the horizon heralded a fine day. It was to prove just that, with hardly a ripple on the blue-grey waters as we cruised majestically north-east. Surely it must be rare for these notoriously stormy waters to be so calm. We had seen no land since early morning, not even a ship. The isolation briefly reminded me of the days and weeks spent steaming across the vastness of the Pacific Ocean some four years earlier.

Just before 9.00 am on the Monday we entered Mauranger fjord and whilst enjoying our free ice-creams and coffee on the games deck at 10.30 am our lovely white painted ship proceeded up Hardanger fjord, although some thirty seven miles long it is nowhere much more than half a mile wide with snow capped mountains rising sheer from the blue green waters which in places plunge to a depth of two thousand feet. The sun shone brilliantly over the distant snow covered mountain peaks. Typical Norwegian houses dot the steep fjord slopes and where the rugged rocks give way to cultivable soil I could see farmers and their wives laboriously hanging fresh cut green grass on a wire fence to dry. Here and there a forage harvester was at work in the larger meadows. It seems like a one man operation, fill a tiny trailer, unhitch the forager, then off down the track to an

Ruth by Clearwater Lake Manitoba

Sunset on Houghton Island, Lac La Ronge Saskatchewan

The magic of Mirror Lake, Pender Island British Colombia

A lone Bristlecone Pine Inyo National Forest, California

A touch of the good life aboard *Canberra*

Sailing off Spitsbergen

Buffalo powered irrigation wheel

Unique mountain scenery down the Li River

undercover silage clamp. A few sheep and cattle graze rough pastures, on the lower slopes. Certainly not farming country as we know it back home.

Twelve noon the ship can go no further, Canberra turns to port and commences to retrace her course. Not wishing to miss any of this magnificent scenery Ruth and I decide on a buffet lunch in the Island Room. The last word in luxury, enjoying a nice meal, easy chairs, good company, looking out through picture windows as we cruise sedately to our next port of call.

Andalsnes. 7.00 am 21st June 1987 we drop anchor. It's raining steadily, low clouds ring the mountain peaks, a dull grey day which gave us a poor impression of this popular resort. Typical wooden Norwegian houses like so many little boxes, their weather-boarded sides brightly painted in a gay variety of colours nestle amongst the trees on the wooded slopes. 8.00 am a call goes out over the ships speakers, "This is the bridge, coxswains man the boats". The launches, already lowered and riding tight to the mother ship await passengers who have booked to go on tours. At the foot of the iron steps leading down from "D" deck, anxious crew members extend a helping hand to us elderly travellers as we step cautiously onto the gunwale of the Canberra's lifeboats. There are seats for thirty passengers but in an emergency each would carry some 120 people.

Ruth and I had decided we would join the intrepid small group on a hike though the mountains, our goal was the high summer pastures. Once ashore passengers were ushered to their respective coaches according to which tour they have chosen. Our group of thirty two, easily distinguished by our hiking boots and waterproofs boarded the first coach which was to drive through the centre of Andelsnes past the octagonal church at Veblungsnes and along the picturesque Romsdalsfjord to Innfjord. At times the mountains drop sheer to the water, the road vanished through well lit tunnels cut through solid rock, some of which must be over a mile long. In a while the road started to climb, twists and turns in hair-pin bends. Here the road branches off through the fertile Innsfjord valley to Berrill. Our driver could take us no further, the road, if you could call it that, had deteriorated to a narrow gravel track. We had two English speaking mountain guides to escort our small party on the stiff climb, it was to take us two hours to reach our destination, 'Bostolen'. It turns out our escorts were in fact mother and son. With a lifetime spent in these high altitudes they are much fitter than us. Soon our little group was spread out, snaking crocodile fashion up the mountain trail. In spite of the gentle rain which spoiled the views we couldn't help but admire the summer flora, delicate ferns, blue, yellow and pink flowers flourish in the damp climate. We then paused by a beautiful lake, it's emerald green water trapped between high mountain peaks rising to almost five thousand feet, their higher slopes still snow covered even in mid summer. Endless small streams trickle across our path, occasionally a larger one has to be crossed by a rickety bridge.

Very wet and rather tired our small party arrived at Bostolen at twelve o'clock. Here we found a typical Norwegian "seter," where the cattle were pastured in the summer. This was one of the few where the milk was still processed. We were more than ready to devote ourselves to the inner man, fortifying our fatigued bodies with a mountain lunch. "Lobchouse," a delicious stew not unlike Lancashire hot pot, flatbrod with blueberry jam, coffee or tea. An interesting experience to sit, eat and talk round a roaring log fire in the company of this Norwegian farming family in their stoutly built log cabin with its mantle of wild grass and flowers growing from the soil encased roof.

The milch cows, mostly brown and white, like red friesians had a large bell hanging from a leather strap around their necks, Swiss style, which continually clanged as they grazed among the

A log cabin in Norway

scrub trees of those high mountain meadows. The farmer's wife called them in for milking with a high pitched "oow-chee oucy oucy ooow chee oucy oucy" at least that was what it sounded like, the cows understood and came obediently!

On a green knoll an old man was patiently getting a very large log fire to burn, enquiring the reason for this I was told that it was mid-summer's day. At midnight, in the semi-darkness before the sun rose again at 3.00 am numerous bonfires would dot the shore and lower mountain slopes. The northern people light huge fires on midsummer's night to celebrate the long hours of daylight.

We took a different trail back to our coach which then transported us back to the jetty where our launch was waiting. Then a speedy crossing of the bay to where the Canberra rode majestically at anchor, from the mast the Norwegian flag of our

99

host country fluttered in the stiff shore breeze. On June 23rd at 18.54 hours Canberra weighed anchor and proceeded seaward along the Ronsdalfjorden and set a course towards the Arctic Circle and Lofoten Island. We were due to arrive in Narvik at 8.00 am three days later.

The Norwegian coastline provides one of the most delightful and varied cruising grounds in the world. The weather like our English climate was unreliable. One extraordinary fact is that the total coastline of Norway, if you include the islands, would be long enough, if straightened out, to encircle the continent of Africa some four and a half times! A land of great Fjords which can run inland for up to 115 miles, incredible depths of water, and often almost vertical cliff walls rising 3000 feet or more from the surface. Every morning Ruth and I enjoyed a buffet continental breakfast, sitting in a comfortable swivel armchair, looking out from the glass fronted Island Room as the Canberra steamed quietly up the broken coastline of northern Norway.

Canberra passed northwards across the Arctic Circle at 16.40 on June 25th, subsequently King Neptune issued all passengers with assigned certificate: "I, Neptune, ruler of the Seven Seas, do hereby welcome to my northern Kingdom and do witness within the confines of the Arctic Circle the presence of honoured guests, Bert and Ruth Houghton, who shall be accorded from this day forward, the 25th Day of June 1987 safe conduct through the Lands of the Midnight Sun, by the Elements and Creatures of the Sea and Ice, Land and Sky, together with the full privileges of all who are of our Circle".

The crossing of this invisible line was taken rather flippantly by most passengers, but Ruth and I felt highly honoured.

Narvik is two degrees above the Arctic Circle but thanks to the Gulf Stream, the port remains open throughout the year. Most other ports of the world, at this latitude, are frozen for much of the year. Here the sun was high above the horizon at midnight from about 25th May to 19th July.

Ruth and I had no desire to spend our day ashore amongst the tourist shops of the city, where everything seemed most expensive, although I thought the beautifully prepared reindeer hides a reasonable buy. Troll (the giant or dwarf of Scandinavian mythology) adorned every tourist shop in vast numbers and by now many will have crossed the sea to England. We chose to take a tour by train which would take us high up into the mountains and to Swedish Lapland.

Ascending to Narvik Myr, we had a splendid view of the Tjotta and Fagernes Mountains before continuing along the Rombaksfjord with the Katterat Mountains rising on our right. The Rombaksfjord with its crystal clear water is a wonderful sight, the train then climbed to the mountain plateau (1600 feet) and passed Bjornfjell, the last station on the Norwegian side before crossing the border into Sweden. In that rocky, barren area much snow still remained, there were no trees and little vegetation. We were told that the reindeer moved in their thousands down to the coast for grazing in the summer. Today only a minority of Lapps move with them, most of these people are now settled on smallholdings.

Stopping at the first station over the border, Vassijaure, a new train crew took over and our route took us on through a bleak section of the National Park. Our final destination was Abisko one of the most popular resorts in Lapland. A tourist station at the Lakeside was our venue for lunch before returning on a different route by coach.

We left Narvik on the high tide at 7.00 pm on 26th June slipping away quietly. There were very few people on the quayside as just another cruise liner took her leave. Time for our evening meal in the Atlantic restaurant. Rocky Peseisa, our waiter, a happy fellow who was always so polite. manoeuvred the chair for Ruth to sit down. Brown delicate fingers selected the pink linen napkin from the wine glass, with a quick flick, in case there should be a speck on it, he deftly placed it across

Ruth's lap repeating the procedure for me, at the same time handing us the menu. Ruth and I perused the fine selection prepared by the chef Alistair Dawson, before choosing, Grouse in White Wine, served with White Grapes and Broccoli Spears, Courgettes Provencale and boiled Potatoes. Compote of Preserved Pears with Ice cream, followed by Coffee and the Cheese Board. Delicious as usual, and we didn't even have to do the washing up afterwards!

Leaving with our table companions John and Sheila Moore we made our way to the Ocean Room, presenting in Cabaret that evening Maria Prado and Jose, a Spanish couple who gave a fabulous performance of the Rumba and other Latin American dances, their gyrations getting faster and faster as the evening progressed. The performance ended at 11.00 pm, time for bed, yet somehow we didn't feel like sleep with the sun still shining brightly overhead. So we relaxed in easy chairs on the promenade deck as the ship steamed between the Norwegian mainland and the massive mountains of Lofoten Islands. For hours we had been passing those barren un-inhabited islands, cold, inhospitable, the lunar like scene silhouetted on the skyline. The sun didn't set but seemed to hang in the sky glowing blood red for a time as we kept watch. Now it was starting to rise again, without the sunset we missed the pleasure of a sunrise.

June 27th 1.15 am. Canberra transient the maelstom and once clear set a north-westerly course towards Spitsbergen. During the night the weather deteriorated. Waking to a full blown gale, the sides of our cabin groaned and squeaked in protest as Canberra swayed from side to side. I'm not the best of sailors and we hadn't crossed oceans for over four years. I just made the bathroom before bringing up last nights grouse. What a waste of good food!

In the next cabin our neighbours were two Welsh ladies. The dividing cabin walls were quite thin, every word could be over heard, they talked incessantly and the swaying of the boat only seemed to spur them on to greater efforts.

Previously we had both agreed that cruising was the ultimate holiday for us, steaming for days across wide oceans, good food, good entertainment, pleasant company, a helpful and friendly crew. One big happy family in fact, sailing to exotic places on the world map. This morning we have second thoughts, surely we can't be stupid enough to pay out lots of our hard earned money just to feel so ill?

During the morning of June 28th 1987 the rough stormy weather abated. In the last twenty four hours Canberra had steamed 487 nautical miles across the Norwegian sea. Ruth and I stepped out on deck very early, the sun of course hadn't gone to bed, it's rays reflect off nearby snow shrouded mountain peaks. We were looking at a cold, barren land yet in a majestic way a very beautiful scene, steaming close to shore, round the top of the island. It was of course Spitsbergen, first discovered in 1196, then lost to the world only to be rediscovered by Barents, a Dutch explorer who named it Spitsbergen, meaning 'sharp peaked mountains'. It is the largest of the Svaltbard group of islands and the most northern permanently inhabited land mass in the world. I have always had a great interest in studying maps of the world and this is one part of the globe I never thought I would get the chance to see.

From April to August the sun gives continued daylight, during the rest or the year from October to February, it is but one long black cold night, save for the beautiful spectacle of the northern lights or aurora borealis which I have had the pleasure of watching with my cousin Harry Houghton in the far north of Canada. We were now sailing off Longyearbyen, capital of Spitsbergen, certainly not a pretty place, slag heaps, pylons and cranes add a brutal aspect to a settlement whose monochrome is broken only by brightly painted Lego-like wooden houses.

In a short while Canberra entered Kongsfjorden, high snow

The Land of the Midnight Sun

covered peaks closed in on either side, the ship now at slow
ahead made for the huge glacier at the head of the fjord. Ice
bergs drifting past get larger and larger. One can see the massive
parts of each berg, yet seven-tenth floats below the water
surface. Each one a different size and shape. One can imagine
the contours of figures or animals in the outlines of the ice.
More excitement follows as seals are sighted feeding close
inshore. They move with such grace and agility in water, but are
ponderous on land.

Canberra slows, now stops completely to let off a launch
taking our mail ashore to the small coal mining community of
Ny Alesund. Here the mail will be franked at the most northerly
Post Office in the world. After the return of the mail boat we
headed cautiously forward once more, right to within a few
hundred yards of the head of this massive glacier where every

few minutes great bergs calve from the slow moving river of ice to thunder with a mighty splash into the frozen sea. On the horizon rose another shoreline, a great un-broken sweep of towering cliff which caught the sun and glowed in emerald and amethyst, a table land of solid ice, forty miles across and two hundred feet high and as we closed, so the colours glowed and became more hauntingly beautiful. The cliffs were dark sapphire, blue and mysterious, paling out to a thousand shades of green. Behind the wide expanse of the ice fields, the bright morning sun reflected off the snow covered pyramid like peaks. The tallest 'Dryglaskikammen' at 4669 feet above sea level rises up and through its ring of clouds. Cameras click incessantly, videos cassette recorders whirl as swarms of exited passengers crowd the decks. I note that even the busy chefs have left their work venturing out on deck to witness this fantastic spectacle, scenery beyond my limited vocabulary to describe to you.

Ruth and I decided on a buffet lunch in the Island Room, from there sitting in the easy chairs we watched the icy scenic landscape pass by within a few hundred yards. Outside on the observation deck a stiff breeze kept the temperature down to 15 degrees centigrade. Because the soil is frozen to a depth of hundreds of feet, there is little vegetation. The only plants to grow are the bush-like polar willow and the dwarf birch. Mammals in this part of the world include reindeer, white fox, blue fox and of course polar bears. The musk ox has now been imported from Greenland, also some seventy odd bird species exist on the Svalbard archipelago.

Now in open sea once more we continued to cruise for another two hours, by now we were beyond latitude eighty degrees north. From the observation deck Ruth, myself and a few other passengers willing to brave the weather, looked out towards the pack ice of the Arctic Ocean, a vast white dome floating on top of the world like a papal skull cap. Its centre, the north pole, lay just six hundred miles away. The ice ahead was

Canberra smashes the ice on the roof of the world

shrouded in thick fog, with visibility poor, it would be dangerous and unwise to proceed further. At this point Commodore Chester gave the order to turn back south. In the whole of his career at sea he had never sailed so far north.

The following morning, June 29th, Ruth and I joined early morning risers on "A" deck. What a surprise awaited us, the vessel had entered Isfjorden. Once more high snow covered peaks rose up from the cold waters. The mountains here are flatter with much scree, like the rest of Spitsbergen there is not a tree or bush to be seen, it is a bleak, barren landscape yet impressively very beautiful. Cruising up the fjord in brilliant morning sunshine Canberra made contact with pack ice at the entrance to Sassenfjorden. With the bows thrusting forward into the foot thick ice, huge cracks appeared but it was obvious the ship would not get through to the foot of the glacier some miles ahead. Canberra reversed out into clear water once more, it wouldn't do to scratch the gleaming white paintwork! Anyway it had caused some mild excitement amongst the passengers on the observation deck.

Turning sharp to port we set course back down the fjord. Since it was then 9.00 am we made for the Island Room. It had been fourteen hours since we last ate. This is the life, Ruth and I both agreed, where else could you sit in luxury chairs and enjoy your grapefruit, sliced melons, cereals etc., and at the same time look out at panoramic views or snow covered mountain peaks just a short distance across the water? Occasionally the coastline was broken by icefields spread out between the peaks with rivers of ice casting colossal chunks of ice into the water. Finally we lost sight of land as the ship set a southerly course towards Tronheim. The wind which by now had turned into a good imitation of a hurricane meant that the clay pigeon or trap shooting which had optimistically been planned would again be cancelled for the day. It is not the high winds that are the problem but the fact it can be dangerous on a swaying deck with loaded shotguns. Pheasants of course fly better in high winds and present more of a challenge to the guns, but at least one is stood on firm ground.

Ruth had joined the sewing class in the meridian room, the ladies were each busy making a sea-serpent nicknamed 'Sid'. He turned out to be quite an attractive cuddly toy. Dark red with cream coloured scales along its back. Possibly a Christmas present for one of the grandchildren in due course.

With shooting cancelled, I walked a mile- four times round 'A' deck. In these seas one cannot help but notice the foam packed waves racing by far below. I dread to think how terrible it must be to hear the order "abandon ship," yet a casual glance upwards is reassuring. Slung above are the gleaming white hulls of the lifeboats, twenty two of them, thirty six feet long, each can carry up to a maximum of one hundred and twenty nine people. They are equipped with an exposure cover, and each boat carries six pints of fresh water and six pints of condensed milk per person, plus flares and morse equipment. Since even experienced seamen can suffer from sea-sickness on a lifeboat, sea-sick tablets are carried. Two of the lifeboats carry radio equipment, there is even a fishing line and six hooks on board for the keen fishermen.

June 30th 0715 hours Canberra lay at anchor in Tronhiem Harbour, having steamed a total distance of 899 nautical miles from Spitsbergen at an average speed of 22.36 knots, so the cruise log informed me. Tronhiem, Norway's third largest city after Oslo and Bergen is situated in a bay in the Trondhiemsfjord. I found it to be a clean and lovely city, the people friendly and helpful and their Cathedral very beautiful and most impressive.

Ruth and I had booked on a tour of ten hours duration which would take us with some fifty more of our fellow passengers to the old mining town of Roros. The pyramids of Egypt, the redwood forests of California, Versailles – and Roros. Despite the great differences, these places have one thing in common; they are all on the UNESCO World Heritage list.

The tour started with a bus transfer from the pier to the railway station where we boarded our train. Passing through the city suburbs the line now starts its upward climb. The view is magnificent out over the fjord and beyond except when we vanished into tunnels cut through the towering mountains all around. The highest point on this railroad is at Bergelsjoen which is 2,165 feet above sea level.

Of our day in Roros, it was raining when we got there, it was still raining when we left. Not surprising since it is reputed to rain eight days a week. Eight days a week we inquired from our local guide? "Yes, twice on Sundays" the joker replied. A run down mining town on such a dreary day is not one of the greatest of tourist attractions, however the old sector preserved as a museum piece I found quite interesting if only to show one the very poor and wretched conditions in which those mining families lived and worked. Tiny dark timbered one-roomed houses, which had no more than the bare minimum of self made furniture and accessories. Small narrow alleyways, a view of the smelting house, the old miners bell in the heart of the town and beyond the huge slag heaps. These are still a reminder from the time of blood, sweat and tears. Our fare for the day's trip of £45.00 each also entitled us to a 'slap up' lunch at the Roso Hotel. One couldn't have asked for more and it certainly made up for the poor weather conditions. Afternoon tea was served on our return train journey to Tronhiem and soon after we were transferred back to Canberra, our friendly, floating five star hotel.

Whilst tired, travel weary voyagers enjoyed a dinner that only the Canberra chefs can put on, our ship steamed down the broken Norwegian coast line to enter Geirangerfjord where at 9.00 am the following day ships launches took passengers ashore who had booked for the overland tour to Eidsdal. Ruth and I both agreed this tour proved to be the most interesting and impressive that we had done in Norway. Our coaches climbed up and up incredibly steep mountain roads, negotiating innumerable hair pin bends, by now we were above the summer snow line, snowploughs had cut through drifts of snow much higher than the coaches even at this time of year. Of course these roads are quite impassable during winter. We now got a wonderful view of the mighty Hellesylt waterfall which cascades into the blue green fjord. After another hour of driving through some of Norway's most scenic mountains we arrived at Europe's deepest lake, 'Hornindalsvannet', with its crystal clear water almost 2000 feet deep. The road continued upwards with nineteen more hairpin bends until we drove across Jolbrua bridge, which spans a 330 foot deep gorge. After stopping for a salmon lunch at the Videseter Hotel, we continued our travels passing several mountain trapped lakes to arrive at Djupvasshytta, then up and up once more to the very top of mount Dalsnibba (4920 feet) and what a view! Snow covered mountains, glaciers, lakes and far below us the Geirangerfjord where the Canberra rode at anchor.

After just fifteen minutes on the mountain top, wonderful views can soon lose their attraction and the wind blew through our light-weight summer clothes. Everyone was only too pleased to re-enter the air-condition coach for the return journey back to our ship.

Bergen on July 2nd was our final port of call. Approached from the sea, Bergen looked a lovely town. Around the harbour cluster the oldest and most picturesque houses, they are jammed packed so closely together it would be unwise to have quarrelsome neighbours. The church of St John tops the summit of its hilly peninsula, and on three sides the seven grey rocky hills covered with trees provide it with shelter. We did a half days coach tour of Bergen and the surrounding countryside. Neat well kept farms dot the fertile valleys. As we drove along I couldn't help but admire the tenacity of those Norwegian farmers to gather their hay crop no matter how hard or often it rained. Dressed in yellow oilskins the farmers and their wives continued to pitch very wet green grass on wire fences to dry out over the next few weeks. A most laborious task but I'm sure the only way to salvage a crop in such a climate .

Once more aboard Canberra a course was set for Southampton some 700 nautical miles away. One more full day to cruise a calm North sea, one more evening to dine, wine and dance to the early hours before docking alongside berth 106 at Southampton on the Saturday morning. I had achieved my ambition to visit the Norwegian fjords and cruise to the land of the midnight sun, with the added bonus that we had 'almost' reached the North Pole.

Whilst waiting our turn to disembark I watched with great

interest as the ship was made ready for the next cruise due to start that very evening. Fully laden lorries queue to unload their cargoes. Deck hands manhandle cardboard containers of every conceivable form of produce and drinks onto roller elevators which span that narrow gap of dirty stagnant water between ship and quay. Water hoses connected to main supplies transfer vast quantities of drinking water that are required for the next voyage despite the fact that the ship has its own desalination plant. Fuel tankers on the quay side line up to fill the diesel tanks, the berth is a hive of activity.

This evening well over a thousand exited new passengers will be joining the Canberra for her next cruise, this time to the sunshine of the Mediterranean, what of the poor, hardworking crew? They have got to do their jobs once more, to wait on, smile, and be polite to another swarm of holiday makers all hell bent on having a whale of a time!!

The Chinese Experience

(I have spelt it in Chinese down the side of this page) Behind the Bamboo Curtain, China, a mysterious, unknown country to most Westerners. Home to more than a billion people, almost a quarter of the world's population. This vast multitude are fed by intensive cultivation of just 7% of the earth's arable land. An enormous task by any standard. Yet, Chinese farmers by the million are doing just that on pint-sized plots which gives the countryside the appearance of a giant patchwork quilt. Gone are the extensive communes of the 'people's revolution' covering several square kilometres and the work brigades who farmed them with little will and even less incentive. The family work unit is back, each member granted one Mu (pronounced moo). 600 square metres or 1/15 of an acre to farm to the best of their ability.

Produce, surplus to quota can now be sold on the 'free' market. This arrangement has put new life into a stagnant agriculture, so different from the corruption and indifference experienced in many other parts of the world. Chinese farmers are the new prosperous elite. Our farming system and theirs are worlds apart, but with the need to feed such a huge population and with such different climatic and social conditions, I found they do a grand job. A trip to China in 1988 was therefore a voyage of discovery, to a land so different from ours it may as well be on another Planet.

It is a part of the globe I had always wished to visit, but never expected the opportunity to arise. I was more than delighted when my wife Ruth and I received an invitation to accompany a farming study tour arranged by 'Farmer's Weekly' in May 1988.

My step-daughter Sue and her husband Roger kindly offered to take Ruth and me to the airport. An early start was called for. Their Range Rover was outside our farmhouse door at 6.30 am. Mist hung low in the valley, but already the sun had risen, casting shafts of light through the still bare oak trees of Mousefield copse. My son Tim was already well through the first milking session of yet another day. Work starts early on a large dairy farm.

We had packed little in the way of luggage, we intended to travel light. China is not a country where one is expected to dress for dinner! As we were driven down the farm drive, I turned and cast a glance at my beloved Mousefield, my home for the past forty-odd years. The white painted pebble-dash walls looked so solid and secure. In a way I was quite sad to be leaving, yet I knew it was not for ever.

Traffic was beginning to build up on the M4 and M25, but we had an uneventful journey to Gatwick arriving there by 8.00 am. In the departure lounge we met our fellow tour companions and Peter Jones of 'Farmer's Weekly', also Michael Miller who was to be in charge of this small group of farmers drawn from various regions of the UK.

Boarding flight number 938, I noted that almost all our fellow passengers were oriental. The diminutive Chinese airhostesses with their oval faces, high cheek bones and button size noses look delightfully pretty in their blue uniforms, hand embroidered petticoats with pink edging and lotus flower motifs. The usual brief formalities completed, seat belts fastened, our plane roared down the runway into a stiff head-wind, climbed and turned to greet the early morning sun. Below, the wooded heathland of the Surrey countryside was soon left well behind. A brief stop was made at Zurich, then again at the United Arab Emirates airport to refuel and change crew.

Next stop Beijing
We landed safely at Beijing International airport at 12.00 local time. Our little group of western farmers and their ladies looked out of place and rather lost, however we soon cleared customs, now to collect our cases. They started to come through on the endless moving belt. Ruth and I waited patiently watching the baggage being whisked away by our fellow passengers. Finally there was none left. Our one and only case had failed to arrive! I contacted a Chinese official and he made enquiries. After a long wait he returned "Velly sorrie, your luggage left behind in Zurich. No problem. Telephone here tomorrow, perhaps case come on next flight, velly sorrie" repeats our little Chinaman. We had arrived in China with just the clothes we stood up in, not even a toothbrush between us! Ruth was almost in tears, why should our case be the one to get lost amongst the hundreds on board? "Never mind love. Shoes, clothes and other essentials are dirt cheap in China so what are you worrying about? The insurance will cover it anyway." In the arrival lounge, after a gruelling seventeen hour flight we were greeted by two guides. A national one who was to accompany us throughout our trip and a local one. Possibly to monitor that we saw only what they wanted us to see. One big plus is that there are few places in the world where you are less likely to have your belongings stolen. Nor are there many places where your

personal safety is more assured. We had to remember that we would be treated as guests in their country and that guests are expected to know how to behave.

Passing through the main airport doors, we stepped out into bright spring sunshine and our first real glimpse of mainland China. Boarding the waiting bus we were introduced to our tour guide Mr Yeng. Who would be known to us in future as 'Edward'.

A young man with a sense of humour and a good command of English. "Good afternoon ladies and gentlemen, I would like to welcome you to the People's Republic of China. There is much to see in this wonderful country of ours, but first I take you to Beijing-The City of the Dragon'. He had lowered his voice and added some mystic.

I was impressed by the luxurious, air-conditioned coach placed at our disposal and the professional skill of the driver as he weaved his vehicle between heavily laden bicycles mostly stacked high with baggage and merchandise of every conceivable description. A coach driver in China is the aristocrat of the road and by government degree has to wear white gloves. Don't ask me why.

The road from the airport cuts through agricultural land, this soon gives way to broad tree lined streets of this large, sprawling metropolis. Beijing is a world-renowned, cultural city with a history of over 3000 years. Covering an area of 16,800 square kilometres, it has a population of over nine million people who travel about their business, work or pleasure on five million bicycles or overloaded public transport. It is a city of contrasts. In densely populated areas dilapidated single story shacks run off the main streets, back to back with the roof of each building almost touching above narrow litter filled alleyways. Whole families live out their lives often in a single room. Sited in the shadows of modern high rise apartments reaching upwards ten, fifteen, twenty stories above the swarms of humanity below. The occupant's daily washing flutters in the breeze from bamboo poles thrust out from each apartment's one and only window.

Some thirty minutes later our coach stopped at a palacious restaurant. The proprietor, obviously expecting us, bowed low and smiling broadly led this mixed bag of English farmers and their ladies to three large circular tables. Around each was placed ten decorative hand painted chairs, the seats of which were much lower than the ones we were accustom to back home and when one sat at the table, ones nose was not far above the level of the soup bowl! In the centre of each table was a large glass dumb waiter heavily laden with a wide range of Chinese cuisine. Whilst on this visit to China, Ruth and I were determined to eat our food only with chopsticks. These most hygienic and civilised implements are a delight to use once the art is mastered. In fact by the time we left the country we had become quite adept in their use and found no difficulty in picking up a peanut or even a few grains of boiled rice from our dishes. They are also one of the reasons that one seldom sees a fat Chinaman, that and the fact that the Chinese either walk or cycle everywhere they travel. Very, very few own a motor car. No monetary payment was made for our substantial meal. We quickly learnt that such minor details were left in the capable hands of our guide Edward. No tips, no gratuities, everything was arranged to simplify our visit to Beijing. Some four hours after landing on Chinese soil we got off at the main entrance of the Friendship Guest House.

Ruth and I slept soundly that night in a luxurious king-size bed, in fact we were both so tired it would have been no problem to have slept on the floor! Early next morning the sun rose red and glowing over the eastern part of Chang'an Avenue. From our hotel window high above the already crowded streets, cyclists pedaled past silently. In contrast the drivers of motorised traffic constantly blew their horns in an attempt to

Rush hour in Beijing

clear a path through a tangle of bikes, rickshaws and pedestrians. Breakfast, Chinese style was a brief affair, although a feeble attempt was made by the chef to serve us with an English breakfast. The ancient fried egg had spread itself over most of the plate, there was some strange beans I couldn't put a name to and the very fat bacon certainly hadn't come from Denmark. As for the toast it must have almost gone up in flames!

8.30 am We sauntered out to our waiting coach. It was a relief to find Edward awaiting us. He smiled broadly as we greeted him, "Neehow", which means "Good morning", the only Mandarin I knew apart from the word for loo! During our visit to China we had two interpreters at our disposal, Edward on permanent duty and a local guide at each new city or commune. Our programme for the next two days would include sightseeing of the national capital, the Forbidden City, the Temple of Heaven, the Summer Palace, the Great Wall and an agricultural visit to a large commune.

China does have traffic regulations, but I got the impression that the only people who know about them are the police, and they, for reasons of their own, keep them a secret. Indeed they seem to spend most of their time yelling at somebody or other through megaphones and giving them a ticking off for no apparent reason. In Beijing, as in many other cities, the streets are clearly marked. There are traffic policemen at the cross-roads and there is a special lane for the swarms of cyclists. There are even pedestrian crossings, but few use them, refusing to believe that motorised vehicles are going to stop. Pedestrians are not deliberately harassed, but the drivers do expect some respect for their superiority. There is a saying in China that the safest way to cross a busy street is to be born on the other side!

Cyclists are not allowed by law to carry passengers. It is therefore not unusual to see a passenger jump off a cycle just before the cross-roads, run across the street past the policeman and then jump onto the bicycle again when he is at a safe distance from the law.

Usually tourists get there first shock in a bus when they notice that in this capacity the driver is king. Because of this they are very self-confident. They wear white gloves as a symbol of their unimpeachable authority and they usually earn more money than most of their fellow citizens. You begin to appreciate the true qualities of your driver once you are outside the city itself. If your journey takes you through country areas then you soon realise that a different set of rules apply. The bus driver has to contend with narrow lanes that are often blocked by convoys of lorries, not to mention the scores of cyclists. The farmers don't help matters either, coming into town with their produce to sell on the free market, often blocking the road with heavily laden three wheeled bicycles or slow moving carts drawn by mules, donkeys or even people. In this latter case you will see the man, bent double pulling in the shafts with his hard working, weary wife pushing at the rear.

If you are of a nervous disposition it is advisable to sit at the back of the bus and only look out of the rear or side windows! Ruth and I made a habit of sitting in the front seat next to the driver. It required iron nerves, but gave an excellent position in which to use our video camera on the move. Our driver did not use any one particular side of the road, he drove wherever there happened to be space and made constant use of the horn to clear a way through. Over-taking or crossing busy road junctions is a certain assurance that the other person will give way first. A game of brinkmanship which demands ice cold nerves.

Meanwhile our coach driver meandered meticulously through the swarms of humanity without mishap, turned into the broad tree lined western end of Chang'an Avenue. The first joggers were out, whilst in the park one could see hundreds of men and women of all age groups who prefer shadow boxing as their daily relaxation from the tensions of city life. Under the directions of masters of the art, they move with deliberate flowing movements which demand so much concentration and inner harmony. Continuing our tour of the city, one couldn't fail to notice the total absence of brightly-coloured advertising signs which most people in the west have come to accept as normal. Illuminating signs at night is therefore seen as wasteful. Electric power is not squandered in this country on the non-essential. With feverish energy the old city slums are being demolished to be replaced by modern high rise flats, the whole project being achieved without mechanical aids. Building sites literally teem with workers of both sexes all clad in identical dark blue overalls and soft cotton caps. English safety inspectors would have a field day prosecuting Chinese building contractors as their workers clamber up steep, slippery planks with a long

Taxi service Chinese style, Tiananmen Square

bamboo pole across their shoulders from which are slung two huge baskets filled to the brim with cement, bricks or whatever. As the new buildings reach for the sky, the shell is encased in a terrace work of bamboo scaffolding held in place by hessian ropes. Scant regard is given to the safety of the workers. Replacements are easy to come by!

The tour coach stopped for the first time on the western edge of Tiananmen Square. Extending over 250 acres (100 hectares), it is indeed a vast open space, four times larger than Moscow's Red Square, our tour guide informed us with much pride. Chinese families strolled in the spring sunshine gazing in wonderment at the Great Hall of the People, which is situated on the west side. It has a meeting hall that can hold over 10,000 people. The southern wing of this building contains a number of small meeting rooms and the offices of the privy council.

Important official receptions and banquets also take place here. High ranking Party officials, state administrators and foreign diplomats arrive and depart in black chauffeur driven limousines. For several years now, the public hall has been open for visitors. Standing at the centre of the square is the Monument to the People's Heroes, an obelisk that bears inscriptions taken from Mao Zedong and Zhou Enlai. Its base is adorned with reliefs depicting various scenes from the revolution. The first thing one can see towards the south is the Mao Mausoleum built in 1977. On the side the huge picture of Mao shows his face with red rosy cheeks, dark eyes, receding hairline even to the wart on his chin which is always shown. Apparently the Chinese consider it brings good luck! Also known as the Square of Heavenly Peace, it is ironic that such a place was to witness such dreadful scenes of violence and hate just one year after our visit.

After a brief stop, we again boarded the coach and continued our tour which included a visit to the Forbidden City, The Temple of Heaven and the Summer Palace. The Palace Museum, known also as the Forbidden City was built between 1406 and 1420 and was the imperial palace of the Ming and Qing dynasties. Ruth, capturing the scene on her video camera was soon partly surrounded by a small crowd of curious Chinese onlookers. They gaped stolidly at this tall, slim European female with an oversized camera resting on one shoulder, right eye glued to the eyepiece and all the while talking to this strange piece of equipment in a foreign tongue. In fact our whole group was the cause of many curious glances. Who are these big, well fed men in tailored suits, wearing collars and ties and sporting size 12 shoes? Men with spade size hands, big ears, big noses and weathered faces looking rather like a russet apple. Their ladies in brightly coloured dresses and a wide variety of head-gear. The two cultures are a whole world apart.

The 'Temple of Heaven', is actually the largest temple

complex in all of China. Extending over 270 hectares, this site is three times the size of the Imperial Palace, but there are few buildings on it. The main structure, a huge pagoda, is the Hall of Prayer for Good Harvests. Most important when there are so many hungry mouths to feed. The temple has a unique circular top covered with blue tiles. A gilded globe crowns the roof. The entire hall was constructed without steel girders or nails. Columns, beams and a complicated system of brackets support the roof. The 28 vermilion columns have symbolic meaning. The four columns standing in the middle are the strongest. They are entwined by golden dragons, which stand for the four seasons. Another twelve columns are spaced around these in a circle, representing the twelve months of the year. The outermost ring of twelve columns are symbolic for the twelve hours of the day. In contrast to present day practice, imperial days were divided into twelve units of two hours each. At the centre of the ceiling are images of a dragon and a phoenix, the symbol for the emperor and the empress.

Finally our daylong tour of Beijing was to take in the Summer Palace. It has a long history, but this is not intended to be a history book I am writing, so I will skip the details. Suffice to say that the 290 hectare site can be divided into two sectors. To the south lies the artificial Kunming Lake. A boat ride takes one past the 150 metre long Bridge of the seventeen Arches and the marble Jade Belt Bridge. As far as the scenery is concerned it is all very beautiful and for us it finished a most pleasant day.

Day two: Edward, always helpful, telephoned the airport. Meaningless chatter was translated for our benefit. Our suitcase had finally arrived and was awaiting collection, but I would have to collect in person. The capital's airport, sited on the outskirts of the sprawling city of Beijing is an hours run from the Friendship Hotel and I didn't fancy travelling on over-crowded public transport. "What about travelling by taxi Edward?" I asked our guide. He threw his arms upwards in a

Edwards written message to the taxi driver

helpless gesture. "Taxi in very short supply, most doubtful I get one." said Edward. "Well you won't know unless you try, get on the phone, go on, give it a go, we want to get our belongings back, you said something about a banquet tonight I will want to wear my suit." I replied. I accompanied him to the one and only hotel telephone. It took an age to get through, but with success at last. Excitement mounted in Edward's voice, "Well, what's the result of all that babble?" I enquired. With a wide grin on his normal bland face, he said, "Taxi come. I tell boss man" .Very important foreign guest require taxi at once." In a few minutes a gleaming, black Japanese built limousine pulled up at the hotel steps driven by a pleasant Chinese lady who couldn't speak one word of English! Instructions to the driver were written out in those strange characters which to me are completely meaningless. Ruth insisted on coming too, no way was she going to see me vanish into this crowded ant-heap of 9 million Orientals. Finally, after being driven through rush hour

Beijing traffic we got to the airport. With the aid of much sign language and our written message our case was produced. The return journey to the hotel was uneventful. It must have been an official taxi because no one asked me for any payment toward the fare!

That evening, the end of our second day in China a traditional banquet was given in our honour. "Important English farmers and their wives must see Chinese people as hospitable hosts", proudly explains our tour guide. A luxurious air-conditioned coach was placed at our disposal. We were driven from our hotel through the poorly lit streets of down-town Beijing. With little private enterprise there is no great incentive to illuminate shop fronts. The roads were still quite crowded with cyclists and pedestrians either going to or returning from their place of work. With such a vast population and virtually no unemployment work continues seven days a week and round the clock. Only by staggering the work force can such numbers move around the city at all.

In due course our coach came to a halt in a narrow, rat-infested side street, disappointment and a certain amount of disgust showed clearly on the faces of our small party. The restaurant looked drab and uninviting. A number of unsavoury looking characters squatting in the street gazed curiously as we disembarked, but once inside all was glitter and gold. We were met at the door by the restaurant manager, who repeatedly bowed almost to the floor. He lead us across the foyer and up a small flight of stairs. Walking silently on plush carpets we were handed over to petite Chinese girls with an alluring beauty who smiled graciously and guided us to our reserved tables.

Food has always been fundamental to the Chinese, more than mere sustenance among the masses. Whilst we were not served bird's nest soup, a Chinese banquet is a great experience. Eight or ten people at each round table were served with as many courses as there were people sitting there. Our meal, which included small appetisers, consisted of assorted meat dishes we couldn't name. Next followed soft wheat and rice-flour noodles cooked with crunchy vegetables. Very complicated rules prescribe the proper order in which individual dishes are served. 'Solid' dishes are alternated with 'soft' ones, spicy with mild, sweet with sour. Poultry will be succeeded by fish and so on through the meal. Rice is served almost last, guests are expected to have had their fill by then. Soup, tasty but wishy-washy, is always the final course. We all persevered with the use of chopsticks with a little more success than of late. In my case it was clear I would not over-indulge. By the time I finally succeeded in getting a tasty morsel to my mouth, the dish was whisked away by an over enthusiastic waitress! To give praise where praise is due, it was an excellent meal far removed from the local Chinese takeaway back home, yet one thing was missing to complete a good meal, no drink was served other than a weak beer. In fact in all my travels through China very seldom did a bottle of wine appear.

The evening for us was far from over, our generous hosts had arranged a visit to the opera. The theatre was most impressive, tastefully carpeted with quiet lighting and raised seating in a huge semi-circle. With a background of Chinese music, we were shown to our seats. In our case our host had dispensed with the formality of tickets.

China is a multinational country and each of it's 55 minority nationalities has its own tradition of song and dance. Movements drawn from animals and birds all form an important part of their dances. To westerners some of the musical instruments played are most weird and the colourful costumes worn by the dancers are out of this world. Most beautiful were the dresses worn by the dancers in 'The saga of a poor farmer's son, who courts and gains the hand of a beautiful princess.' The story leads up to 'Sending the Bride to the Groom's Home', 'The Bride's Journey' reflects the Yugur's unique marriage customs. For energy expended, nothing was to equal 'The Bullfight', a dance of the Daur people, who live in the Inner Mongolian Autonomous Region or the 'Joyful Threshing Ground' which depicts rejoicing over a bumper harvest. It was all very colourful and Ruth managed to capture quite a lengthy part of the evening on her video camera, which we hoped would prove interesting to folk back home. The fact that all the words and music was gibberish to us, did nothing to spoil our enjoyment of the evening.

Places in China have wonderful names. I was intrigued at the outset by the 'Hall of Supreme Harmony', 'Palace of Heavenly Purity', 'Palace of Earthly Tranquillity', 'Gate of Divine Wisdom', 'Gate of Dispersing Clouds', 'Hall of Joy and Longevity'. The lovely names go on and on. There is even a 'Hall of Enjoyment'. But since I didn't get to visit that one I am afraid I cannot tell you what form of pleasure was enjoyed there!

May 8th 1988 6.00 am

The City of Beijing was awake, in fact it really hadn't slept at all, activity continued non-stop. I was wide awake at 6.00 am. The sun had risen, casting shafts of silver rays through the trees outside our hotel balcony. With limited motorised traffic, the streets appear quiet, but the early morning workers are out in their thousands. Looking down at the scurrying multitude, such frenzied activity reminds me of a disturbed ant heap. I made two cups of jasmine tea using boiled water supplied overnight in a large, beautifully decorated flask, it is unwise to drink or clean one's teeth from water that 'sometimes' comes out of the bathroom taps.

Breakfast at 8.00 am. We cross the street to building No.1. Once again each group of ten sit around a circular table. Promptly a continental breakfast is served. Toast (which this time was only warmed bread) and boiled eggs, followed by more 'toast' and surprise, surprise, strawberry jam. Dairy products are always in short supply, one rarely sees butter, and fresh milk is non-existent, yet I must admit that milk would ruin the taste of the many flavoured blends of Chinese tea. However, what would I have given for a good old English breakfast of fried bread, two thick rashers, a few mushrooms and a fried egg! The meal over, I made enquiries from an English speaking waiter as to the possibility of finding a foreign exchange bank. The directions he gave to me meant a walk of perhaps a kilometre through rush hour traffic. Luck was with me, I found the bank and the teller spoke some English. Exchanging £60 I received something over 400 yuan, that is seven yuan to the £1. I made my way back to the hotel, my wallet stuffed with small denomination notes reminiscent of monopoly money. Unfortunately I hadn't realised how long my walk to the bank and back had taken. Everyone of our party was already aboard the coach, the white gloved driver sitting at the wheel with the diesel engine ticking over. Edward was most aggrieved by the delay and laid down the law on passengers upsetting his strict time schedule. He had planned a visit to the Ming Tombs and the Great Wall, it was to be a long day.

Edward counted his 'sheep' once more, numbers now correct. Quick fire instructions to driver who swings the coach out of the hotel precinct into Baishiquias Road, ahead is an extremely busy cross-roads. The policeman stood in the centre on a small red box. With blasts on his whistle and frantic waving of white gloved hands he attempts to bring some sort of order to the scene. Chinese in their thousands hurry on their way, pedestrians, cyclists, buses and electric trams in tandem each one jammed solid with humanity. En-route Edward gave a running commentary:- "On your right ladies and gentlemen, is very important building 'China Art Gallery'." I looked out on the wrong side of the coach and missed the site. Never mind there were plenty more impressive buildings to see. Next

Edward asked a question of us. "How many Chinese people can stand on a square metre? You don't know? I will tell you. Twelve, but perhaps not so many over-fed Europeans!"

Leaving the suburbs we stop off to visit the Ming Tombs, situated some 50km north-west of Beijing at the foot of the Tianshousham Mountains. Thirteen Ming Emperors, their wives and concubines were buried here one after the other from 1368-1644. The valley opens up into the Plain of Hebei to the south where the Dragon and Tiger mountains form a natural gateway to the burial site. On our way we drove through intensively farmed areas, fertile, flat and very productive. Dry rice was growing in long narrow strips and at this period in its growth, was about18 inches high. Edward, our courier, informs us that it is cut by hand when harvested. Every possible inch of ground is cultivated, definitely no question of set-a-side in this part of the globe! Our coach driver used the horn almost continuously in his efforts to clear a path through heavily congested country roads. Mainly farmers making for the free markets of Beijing. Three wheeled bicycles draw heavily laden two-wheeled trailers piled unbelievably high with every conceivable object. 12 H.P diesel 'walking' tractors transport dung, bricks, timber, crates of livestock and just about everything else. Two, often three boney, scraggy mules pull huge loads of miscellaneous farm produce. I noticed these same mules had a 'nappy' slung between the two shafts of the rubber tyred cart, this to catch any droppings which were far too valuable as fertiliser to be allowed to fall on the road for some other person to collect free for their small plot of land, also the other bonus was that this method kept the streets clean!

After a brief stop for lunch we continued our journey northwards climbing steadily through the foothills of the vast range barring the route to Inner Mongolia. Our destination, perhaps the highlight of our travels through China, was the Great Wall. This wonder of the world winds its way over vast territories from the banks of the Yalu River, to end at the foot of snow-covered Qilianshan and Tianshan mountains. It extends for 6,350 kilometres through nine provinces and according to astronauts who looked back on earth from the moon, it is the only man-made project that can be clearly seen. Still climbing, the coach rounds a long left hand bend, there on the shoulder of the next mountain we got our first view of this man-made defence line. Like a great dragon, it twists, curves, rises and falls to finally disappear over some distant peak.

We were given a time limit of two hours to walk part of the wall. Ruth and I chose the eastern section, which our Queen had walked the year before, but I'm sure the swarms of oriental tourists were kept at bay on her official visit. The trouble is that only a tiny part of the wall is open to the public, which means that it gets terribly over-crowded and for me this ruined the pleasure of walking along the crest from one beacon tower to the next. Looking north over mist topped mountain ranges, we were viewing the vast almost uninhabited land of Inner Mongolia. Climbing higher, in places up long flights of stone steps, the crowd thinned as we got further and further away from the coach parked far below. What is not always realised is that the Wall is really a series of border defence works built, dismantled and re-built over a period of more than two thousand years. More than twenty walls have been built in some sections as reinforcement.

The Chinese have a saying. "If you haven't walked the Great Wall, you haven't lived." I wouldn't entirely agree, but nevertheless it is a great experience, one that I will always remember.

On the long return journey our coach driver had to negotiate country roads, still choc-a-block with traffic even though it was getting late in the day. Rounding a blind corner, Ruth and I almost shot through the windscreen when our driver did an emergency stop. Slap-bang in the middle of the road was an ancient looking Chinese farmer who had two very energetic, long-haired bacon-size pigs roped firmly onto an old door, which in turn was secured to the rear carrier of his bike. What a field day our RSPCA representative would have if farmers back home arrived at our local market using this form of transport!

We returned to the capital via Deshengmenwai Street which crosses over the outer city ring road, then over the bridge spanning the narrow neck of water between Xihai Lake and Houhi Lake before continuing southwards past four more lakes, although this picturesque area of water is in reality one long continuous stretch of water. Most members of our group were showing the effects of a long strenuous day, but a brief 'courtesy' stop and a drink of jasmine tea put new life into everyone. Back at our hotel, we were given one hour to wash and change. Tonight our hosts had arranged something extra special – a banquet at the famous Beijing Roast Duck Restaurant. What an evening that turned out to be. These Chinese feasts were not just dinners, they were more of an endurance test 10, 12 courses or more. We waded through birds nest soup, fried frogs legs, steamed octopus and of course the renowned Roast Duck, to mention but a few. All washed down by some strange drink that was supposed to resemble English beer. My stomach had been raised on grilled steak and baked potatoes, so the sudden change of diet was not always appreciated! Believe you me, the Chinese chefs back home have a lot to learn.

Next day I had great difficulty in getting myself mobile. After last night's celebrations a day of rest would not have come amiss. However our itinerary was about to give us our first direct contact with Chinese farmers. We were due to visit the Sijiqing (Evergreen) Township which is located in the Haidian District of west suburban Beijing. On arrival we were greeted by important members of the organisation. Introductions, bowing and hand-shaking over, we were escorted to the beautifully

Farm mechanisasion. The Sijiqing (Evergreen) Commune

decorated tea house. Sitting at long, low tables with polished glass tops, we were served steaming hot herbal tea in tiny ornate cups. Through our interpreter we were given a summary of the Township's products.

The following brief statistics gives some idea of the vast difference between an English farm or even a large country estate and a Chinese commune. Sijiqing with an area of 72.6 square kilometres, has a population of 46,000 people of whom 26,000 are working. It is large and profitable and, as a result, its inhabitants enjoy a standard of living better than most. Its location has a lot to do with this prosperity. Close by the western suburbs of capital City Beijing, it has an insatiable market on the doorstep ready to gobble up everything it produces. With some 2400 hectares (5930 acres) of farmland, it takes its Evergreen name from the fact that 1460 hectares (3600

131

acres) are down to vegetables sold fresh in the City all year round, 530 hectares (1310 acres) to fruit and the remaining 990 acres growing grain, mainly wheat. Such a large area under extensive cropping and with very little mechanisation, there is of course work for everyone, especially bearing in mind that a lot of the land produces three crops each year. One must also be aware of the fact that diversification is not something that only happens on English farms. On this commune we were told that 27 companies engaged in such diverse undertakings as brewing, processing leather, chemicals, building and machinery maintenance.

Apart from two technical schools, one agricultural and one industrial, there are 20 primary schools and six secondary schools, as well as kindergarten and nurseries-for almost 10,000 children.

Our visit to the dairy herd was an eye-opener. The 300 dairy cows are kept in yards American style. In all, 90 people work in and around the unit, 32 of them hand-milking the herd three times a day 5.00 am to 8.00 am, 11.30 am to 2.00 pm, and 6.00 pm to 8.30 pm. Not, I would add, because of a tremendously high milk yield (average 600 gallons per lactation), but more to keep the huge staff in work.

The head-to-head yoke-tied byre with centre feed passage, where the cows are not de-horned to prevent them from slipping out of their yokes, had an over-head vacuum pipe-line for mechanical milking. But it was not in use due, we were told, to the unreliable electricity supply. Another team of workers moved around the open yards scooping up the cowpats for recycling through the vegetable plots, and 'night soil' from the human population is another form of fertiliser that is never wasted.

Piggeries and chicken houses lay side by side, yet I must say I was far from impressed with the porkers being produced from the horrid looking black, pot-bellied Chinese sows. Then there are 11 acres of water producing fish and turtles, all these enterprises are very labour intensive yet they make plenty of work for what would otherwise be idle hands. Average wage at that time was 2300 yuan (£330 per year,) double what the city worker received a few miles down the road in Beijing. People can choose to stay at home and work their own plots or work on the main commune and get paid accordingly. Most do both I discovered.

Out in the fields they produce two grain crops a year from the same land. Wheat and rice with a combined tonnage of often 20 tons per hectare. Every square inch of land is fully used even to the extent of two rows of broad beans planted on the headland furrow around each wheat field. But unlike the Western world awash with surpluses, some foodstuffs are still rationed in towns and hunger is never far away.

Muscle power is paramount, there's no other way for most. Chinese farming folk are immensely strong. Men and women often carry more than their own weight by yoke and pannier arrangement, often at a half run and they also pull fantastic loads on two-wheeled carts. I've seen them moving along country lanes with long concrete slabs, timbers or drain pipes up to ten metres long held in place by hessian ropes. Hand tools and man ploughs are common enough. The more affluent may have a water buffalo or a pair of mules to supplement their own muscle power. You are really with it if you own a single-cylinder 12HP 'walking' tractor. On thousands of miles of internal flights and long distant train journeys zigzagging across that vast country, I never saw one decent size field as we know them in this part of the world, just plot after plot as far as the eye could see. Nor did I see more than a score of what we would call a medium-size tractor in the 50-60 HP class, and these were on the roads. There are just no fields large enough to work them and in any case if there were, they would replace too much manpower. The Chinese say an inch of land is worth an inch of gold, with that fact in mind even odd corners of a field or under power line poles where the drill cannot reach, are hand dug and planted with some edible crop. On our train journeys, Chinese peasants worked beside the rails up to within a couple of metres of the speeding trains, growing and harvesting barley, oil seed rape, potatoes or such like. Through our interpreter I put a question to a farmworker. "Do you have a lawn to your house?" Came back the reply: "No, every piece of land must be tilled, there's none to spare just to sit on!" Our day had been hard yet very educational. We were all much, much wiser on Chinese farming practices and I could only congratulate them on what was obviously a great lesson in self sufficiency.

The next day, after another early breakfast we were driven to Beijing airport, where we boarded a small prop-driven plane which, after a bumpy take off, headed inland. The pilot flew very low across country. Flat, fertile land, heavily cropped and drained by the many tributaries of the Yellow River flashed below. I had the impression that our pilot had previously been employed on air-craft crop spraying before he changed to civilian flights, the way he skimmed the contours. He seemed to navigate visually following one river system after the other. The air stewardess came round offering sweets, more to calm our nerves and reduce the ear-popping caused by the lack of air pressure control, than as a form of refreshment!

Two hours later to everyone's immense relief we landed at Xi'an airport. Xi'an (pronounced Shee-an) the capital of Shaanxi Province and the biggest city in the north-west of this vast country. It has a history of over 3000 years and here one can visit The Banpo Museum, The Bell Tower, Wild Goose Pagoda, The Huaqing Hot Spring and of course the famous Terra-cotta warriors. Over 6,000 life-size figures of soldiers and horses in perfect battle array showing the superb sculptural art of that time.

The world famous Terra-cotta army has made this city a

tourist resort, but it has always been an important centre in that it was the starting point of the well known 'Silk Road' which linked the East and West in early trading days, when a journey from Europe was reckoned in months and years rather than so many hours plane flight. Today you no longer have to face arduous adventures, endless expeditions across mountain ranges or deserts, or undertake dangerous sailing trips in order to reach China. You can fly there from London in twenty hours or less.

The Warriors and Horses of Emperor Qin Shi Huang which were buried more than two thousand years ago, caused a sensation throughout the world since they were unearthed early in 1974 by some Chinese farmers digging a well. 720,000 people worked for 37 years to make these warriors.

Beautiful, well maintained rose gardens line the approach to a huge domed building built to protect the grave site from the elements. As one enters (no cameras or videos allowed), the first thing the visitor sees is a formation of men in three columns, made up of marksmen, archers and crossbowmen. Directly behind them stand six war chariots. Each chariot is drawn by four horses and manned by a charioteer and two soldiers. Behind these war chariots there are eleven corridors of men. In nine of these the infantry stand four abreast. In the two outer lines the soldiers posted on the flanks, stand facing outwards, in that way protecting the troops from a flank attack. Officers can be distinguished from the ranks by their clothing and equipment. What really impressed me was that no two faces are exactly alike. All the figures are life size and we were told measure between 5'7" and 6'1". They were originally painted and carried real weapons, but over the centuries the paint peeled off or faded owing to the ravages of time. Since 1979, most of the figures have been restored and displayed in Pit No.1 at the original position. A series of chariots were put in order with great boldness and vision. With their heads raised and chests expanded, all the warriors are full of vigour and life, with expressions different from each other, while the horses with heads raised, ears pricked, eyes and mouths open wide, look for all the world like neighing and ready to gallop at any moment. The hard grey clay that the figures are made of comes from the area surrounding the Li Mountain. This material made it possible to form such large figures, which were then fired at high temperatures. None of the soldiers have helmets, yet it is noticeable that each battalion wear different hair styles.

The second site contains a cavalry unit consisting of more than 1,400 warriors and horses. In addition to the spearmen, archers and armoured cavalrymen, 64 war chariots were exposed, also their two commanders were found. Yet even today only about one tenth of the site has been excavated by archaeologists. It is truly a most spectacular sight to see rank after rank of such life-like figures still silently standing, after over 2,000 years. One can scarcely imagine the splendour created by this terra-cotta army in their original brilliance, every minute detail absolutely correct. I had of course seen pictures and read about these figures, but I was not prepared for the sheer vastness of this life-sized army which some claim to be the eighth wonder of the world.

Back again in the City with a couple of hours to spare before supper, Ruth and I decided we would take a bus tour. We had been told that a ride on a public bus was quite an experience and for five Fen (two pence) one can stay on the bus for as long as you wish. Once aboard however the problem is to get off the blessed thing. It's bad enough getting on the bus unless you are good at pushing and shoving, but by the time the already crowded vehicle has made a few more stops, you have been squeezed into a solid mass of humanity somewhere in the centre. It's no good saying, "Excuse me, please can you let me through?" No one understands and you are met by stony, uncompromising stares. Despite the cramped conditions, we saw a large section of the City wall. One has to be amazed by the grandeur of this immense construction. Built in the Ming Dynasty, it circles the city and is the longest city wall in the world. We did manage to de-bus at the main shopping centre which had some quite nice shops, although window dressing even in the small privately owned shops leaves much to be desired.

Next day we flew to Nanjing by C.A.A.C (which incidentally our Chinese guide told us jokingly stood for 'Chinese airways always cancelled'). Information in the airport lounge was of course in Chinese. We all sat placidly, there was no rush, we would all move like sheep when our plane arrived. Surprisingly it landed on time coming to a halt some 300 metres from the terminal building. The small twin-prop military aircraft had been laid on specifically for our use. Edward was still with us and proudly he lead his charges across the concrete runway to the waiting plane. An army truck shot past us, our luggage thrown haphazardly in the back with two civilians sitting atop. All this time both engines had been ticking over, the propellers still rotating, surely against all the rules of safety. A metal step-ladder was pushed into position by two uniformed soldiers. Once everyone was seated, safety belts fastened, the pilot turned his craft into the wind and without more ado gave both engines full rev and soared steeply into a cloudless sky. Far below the chequered pattern of intensive cultivation spread out like a vast map where hundreds of ant-like figures slaved at the endless task of producing food for the masses. Our flight crossed three great provinces Shaanxi, Henan and Anhui, a journey of over a thousand kilometres. During this long flight no meals were served, but each of us was presented with a small present of decorative artwork, two plain biscuits and a cold drink. After a safe landing once again the metal steps on wheels were pushed into position and even as we disembarked, two Army oil tankers were refuelling the plane for its return flight.

Nanjing, meaning 'Southern Capital' in Chinese is one of the oldest cities in China. Since ancient times it has attracted countless Chinese and foreign travellers with its long history and beautiful scenery. With a population of over 4.5 million it is ideally situated for trade on the lower reaches of the great Yangtze River. And what a river! From its source in Tibet, the Yangtze flows through nine provinces. It is the third longest river in the world and has over 700 tributaries.

At times the Chinese can be most proficient, a coach thoughtfully placed at our disposal was awaiting our arrival. We were driven to Xinjiekou Square and here we picked up a new local guide, Mr Ling, who's first name sounded rather like Jimmy so the unanimous decision of our group was that in future Jimmy it would be. His English proved excellent and he informed us that we were the first UK farmers he'd had the pleasure to escort. Of course, we still had our indispensable Edward with us.

Whilst in Nanjing, we enjoyed the luxury of the Jinling Hotel, one of the most magnificent hotels in China, which still preserves age-old Chinese traditions. Pretty girls tapped gently at our door, entered and asked to be allowed to turn our bed covers back and put slippers, thoughtfully provided by the hotel management, on our feet! Our room girl spoke passable English. "Tonight you and lady go in lift to 36th floor, right to top hotel, velly good food, special for Jingling Hotel. Music for dancing, best orchestra in Nanjing, sometimes play English music, and all time top floor slowly turning, in one hour see all of City." Bowing graciously she glided silently from the room.

Tonight Ruth and I teamed up with Maurice and Mary Hassel, two of our party who farm south-west of Bath. They were grand company and both enjoyed a good laugh. The excellent meal which followed was by courtesy of our Chinese hosts, but we were asked to pay an entry fee of £1.50. A beer cost 4.5 yaun 50p. Coffee priced at 10 yaun is rather dear in comparison, however the total bill was only 71.50 yaun. £10. Not too outrageous for four people! We ate, drank and danced 'til midnight before retiring in a rather exhausted state. I realised at this point there were precious few hours until day break, the Chinese are early risers and we had a heavy programme on the morrow, there was much to see in this beautiful city, Edward told us.

Friday the 13th of May 1988. Nanjing 7.00 am.
The sun was already clear of the roof tops to herald a hot day ahead.

Breakfast was at 7.30 am. Edward appeared, he was in a jovial mood. "Please all ready to board coach at 8 o'clock, Mr Ling has big programme for English farmers today." Once on board, our driver headed south for a tour of the City. Interesting buildings and sites were pointed out to us. Bailuzhou Park, Confucious Temple, Rain Flower Terrace; someone inquired of the name. Legend has it that when the famous monk Yunguang sermonised here, even the God was deeply moved, so that flowers fell from the heavens like rain, hence the name.

First stop was at Doctor Sun-Yat-sen Mausoleum which is situated on the southern slope of the Purple Mountains in the eastern suburb of Nanjing. Doctor Sun-Yat-sen was born of a peasant family yet was determined to free the Chinese people from oppression. It is a long story which in the end succeeded in the famous 1911 Revolution. It was a beautiful spot. In the foreground of the Mausoleum was a marble gate of three arches, behind a 480 metre avenue lined with beautiful trees. The memorial hall itself was approached by climbing 392 steps. I can vouch for the number. I counted them! It was quite a climb but well worth the effort.

The highlight of our visit to this part of China was to see and cross the mighty Yangtze River by way of the bridge, a bridge that has turned a natural barrier into a thoroughfare. This monument to Chinese tenacity and skill is a double-decker rail and road link which took eight years to build. The upper deck is a four lane high way, beneath, the double track railway section. When there was no direct overland link between the north and south, the train had to be ferried across. What used to take two and a half hours now takes only five minutes! Approaching from the northern bank our coach stopped for us to get off giving everyone a chance to take photos. It is difficult to fully appreciate the Herculean efforts put in by thousands of Chinese workers to create what is sometimes described as yet another wonder of the world.

Day and night in the silt laden river far below a continuous stream of traffic plies this artery of central China. From giant barges pushing two, three or four heavily laden pods, to the humble family junk. Pleasure cruisers were few and far between, this is a country where work comes before leisure.

May 14th.1988
Our itinerary was to include a journey by train from Nanjing to Wuxi (pronounced woo-see). The Chinese with their huge reserves of coal still rely to a great extent on steam locomotives and a train journey is one of the major experiences of any tour throughout China. We arrived at the station at midday yet the train was not due in until 1.57 pm. Being classed as VIP's we were to be favoured with a soft seat coach and as such enjoyed a fairly respectable waiting lounge, although no refreshments were available. The masses who all required a permit to travel were not so fortunate. Herded like sheep behind steel barriers they could do no more than wait patiently until the train steamed in. When the gate was opened by a platform attendant a stream of humanity rushed the coaches, coaches that were already filled to bursting point. Inquisitive slant-eyed faces peered from closed windows as the little group of Europeans made their way through the crush for the first coach. Edward

marched ahead waving his small Union Jack flag with gusto, anxious not to loose any of his charges. Any mistake on his part and no doubt his rather lucrative job would be at stake. Would-be passengers pushed, shoved and fought to get aboard although riding atop of coaches as in India has now been barred. The amount of luggage some people carried was just unbelievable, huge cardboard boxes, wicker baskets, clothing material, carpets, some even had livestock like a few chicken or ducks. Parents dragged or carried children, it was a chaotic scene.

Seats numbering 4 to 37 had been reserved for us, the coaches were large and whilst not up to British Rail standard they were quite adequate, and all the while harmonious music issued forth from hidden speakers. Chinese trains travel at a relaxed leisurely pace and our route took us through mile after mile of densely cultivated farm land. Our guide explained that these days only two crops are grown consecutively each year due to the extra labour required to cultivate three crops per year as in the past. I couldn't believe they were really short of man power!

Ruth was busy on the journey with her video camera capturing on film the rural scene. Peasants working knee-deep in water planting rice seedlings, hoeing weeds by hand between drills of wheat or doing their best to urge on a reluctant water buffalo pulling a single furrow beam plough. The light was failing when our train finally came to a halt amongst a cloud of white steam at Wuxi main station. Tired and hungry we stepped from the carriage down a flight of three steps. Because we had been in the front coach we had some two or three hundred metres to walk to the soft seat lounge. Crowds of Chinese were rushing past us in the opposite direction their objective to board the train which in my way of thinking was already full to capacity. We were not kept waiting for long . A coach arrived to transport us to the Hubin hotel. Our room number 511 was on the fifth floor with a splendid view of this city of 800,000 souls.

May 15th 1988 5.00 am

Dawn broke. It was overcast and mist hung low over the city streets, but a fine sunny day was forecast. This part of China enjoys a mild climate with fertile soil and a richness of natural produce. 7.30 am Breakfasted on two boiled eggs per person, coffee or tea. We were very westernised that morning, knife and a fork instead of the usual chopsticks. Our group assembled at the hotel entrance. Edward and a local guide checked on numbers, all correct, we seemed to be a well disciplined bunch and I hadn't been late again! Our coach drew in on time. Ruth and I took our usual front seat, there was no great rush for this position. It takes strong nerves and a placid nature to stand a two and a half hour journey looking down other road users necks. Our destination was the village community of Huazi a hundred miles from Wuxi in central China. I thought that when we reached open country we would be clear from traffic. Not likely, the roads were crowded with transport of every description. Ancient lorries, many in the last stages of useful life and over-loaded with manufactured goods, endless streams of farmers commandeered the middle of the road seated on their small diesel one stroke tractors, pedestrians and an endless assortment of two and three wheelers jammed the highway as we passed through numerous villages. Every conceivable item, it seemed, could be carried on a pedal cycle, ranging from 5 or 6 layers of chickens in baskets to a batch of white table ducks, prevented from flight by being tied down by their feet.

I was amazed that literally every square inch of this fertile delta of the Yangtze is cultivated and cropped with vegetables or grain. Wheat is harvested mainly by hand labour in June then the land is flooded to be followed by a rice crop harvested in September.

By the almost ceaseless use of the horn and frequent use of the brake our driver arrived at our destination without mishap.

First we were introduced to the managerial staff of the commune, then escorted to the tea house where the inevitable Jasmine tea was served. There are no tea cups, here tea is drunk from traditional tea bowls, beautifully hand painted and covered with a lid. To drink you lift the bowl with one hand raising it to your lips, lift the lid slightly with the other hand and sip the hot revitalising liquid noisily. If you want your bowl refilled you simply place the lid on the table next to the bowl. You will be brought hot water without having to speak a word. If you leave the table but plan to return, simply put a few tea leaves on the lid. It was during this tea session that the aims and statistics of the commune were explained in great detail giving us the opportunity to compare the wide gulf between East and Western farming methods. I queried the pig unit manager's figure of producing 1,500 pork and bacon pigs per year when he said through the interpreter, "that they had 37 breeding sows". Unabashed he explained that almost a thousand weaners were purchased each year from neighbouring villages.

I was pleased when it was suggested that we all move outside to commence our conducted tour of the commune, one can get bogged down with facts and figures and there is a limit to the number of bowls of tea that one can consume! It soon became apparent that for the Huazi villagers it was boon time yet there was no denying it was the factories and not the farm that had allowed the village to prosper. The boss man Mr. Zhu Yu Liang, pointed to the recently built houses with free running water. Every home had a telephone, a television set and a washing machine. Medical care was free; so was schooling. It has been a big step for them from poverty to what is still virtually peasantry and their own special industrial revolution. Allocation of land can vary in size of plot and quality in different parts of the country but in general every member of a family gets one Mu at birth for their own family use. At first it would appear that the larger the family the more land would be acquired, but it is not that simple. Birth restrictions are very severe and allow only one child per couple except in some more remote areas. Also women must not marry before their twentieth birthday and the men their twenty-second. No having babies at age 16 or 17 to get yourself a flat. Irrigation plays a big part in the growing of such splendid vegetable crops. Alongside a river bank water buffalo were circling endlessly to work pumps lifting water which then flowed into man-made open canals for hundreds of metres. I took a turn to squat on the wooden seat to keep one of the reluctant beasts on the move with a short leather whip. Ruth did a stint on a man or a women powered treadmill which also lifted water for irrigation. Rather amusing for a short spell, but not a job I would favour all day and everyday thank you!

On our return to the City time allowed for what turned out to be a most interesting visit to the silk-worm factory. I did make a few written notes as we toured the gardens and works. This very briefly is the story of silk. In meticulously cultivated orchards of mulberry bushes a small army of workers pick the choice leaves one by one placing each leaf carefully into baskets. This work must be done early in the morning whilst the dew is still on the plant. The mulberry leaf is the only diet of the silkworm which in turn is the larva or caterpillar of a moth, "Bombyx mori". This insect, like all other moths, passes through four stages of life, egg, caterpillar, pupa or chrysalis and finally a perfect insect. The female moth lays from 200-500 eggs on rice straw prepared for her. After the eggs are laid they are placed in trays and incubated at about 72 degrees F, hatching in about ten days. When the worms hatch out, they are only about an eighth of an inch long but they have large appetites and are soon eating their own weight in mulberry leaves daily. They undergo four moults before they are fully grown, the process takes about four weeks. At last, when they are three to three and a half inches long, plump and greyish white in colour, they stop eating and are ready to spin the silken cocoon which serves as a protection when the larva cast off the final skin and becomes helpless pupa or chrysalis. The caterpillars climb supporting strands of straw placed for them. The silk material (fibroin) is formed in glands on either side of their bodies, and two threads issue from an opening in the head called the spinneret. The threads are joined together and are surrounded by a sticky gum which is produced by more glands near the spinneret opening. The fluid threads harden at once in the air, then the larva weaves them into the cocoon completely surrounding its body and attached to the support. The spinning process takes two or three days, and each oval cocoon contains 500 to 1000 metres of continuous thread.

If it were left to itself, the chrysalis inside the silk cocoon would complete the metamorphosis and become a moth, which would eat its way out through one end of the cocoon. Neither the male or female moth is able to fly, and they live only a few days, during which time the female lays her eggs. If the moths emerge from the cocoon they spoil them for spinning, so only sufficient for breeding are allowed to emerge. The remainder are killed by dry heat or steam, inside the cocoons which are then soaked for a few minutes in hot water, to soften the gum. There are always eight cocoons in the water at any one time, the problem is to find the real end. The strand of silk is so fine that it is almost invisible to the naked eye. Today this task is done by a clever piece of machinery. Then the ends of the thread are brought together and through a tiny guide like the eye of the needle. The fibres are then wound together to form a single strand of great strength which is wound upon a reel. When the reel is full, the silk is taken off in large hanks, and this is the form in which most raw silk reaches the factories. It takes, I was told between, 2,000 and 5,000 cocoons to produced a pound of reeled silk. Before the silk is ready to be woven on the loom it has to go through a process called throwing. The raw silk is soaked in an oil emulsion to soften it, then several threads are twisted and doubled into a more substantial yarn. After the silk has gone through several processes it is bleached and dyed. Silk was originally treated with natural dyes such as indigo, cochineal and logwood, but today synthetic dyes are used and they have to be fast to light and to washing.

At the end of the conducted tour the Chinese make sure one cannot escape without passing through the factory shop where one is tempted to purchase silk fabrics and manufactured items at ridiculously low prices. Ruth purchased some silk fabric and two beautiful head scarves. I came away with a couple of silk shirts and enough neckties to be able to wear a different one every day for a fortnight, these last items at less than £1 each!

The Great Canal flows through the town of Wuxi from the north-west in a southerly direction. A network of several smaller canals criss-cross the various districts of the town. With its total length of 1,794 km from Beijing to Hangzhou it is one of the world's largest artificial waterways. A boat journey through the town of Wuxi on the Grand Canal is an ideal way of enjoying the busy scenes of life on the waterway. It takes one past old junks and magnificent arched bridges. Old houses with steps leading down to the water's edge line the route of the canal and women are to be seen washing clothes and sometimes even vegetables, but by the colour and smell of the water one wonders whether the end product was improved by their efforts.

The next day we reluctantly took our leave of Wuxi travelling once again by train. Carriage number 12, our seats reserved. First stop Suzhou where we spent a few pleasant hours before making Shanghai the following day.

Suzhou is situated south of Wuxi and on the banks of the Grand Canal. The first European traveller to discover Suzhou was Marco Polo and apparently he was enthralled by the place. Fortunately, some of the atmosphere and excitement of the town that fascinated Marco Polo has survived to the present day. The narrow streets, the white washed houses with black tiled roofs, tiny front gardens and small narrow pavements all contribute to the special atmosphere. In fact much of Suzhou's claim to fame rests on its magnificent gardens. Ruth and I were most impressed by the Lui Garden, I believe it is the largest in the City. One walks through this garden clockwise, passing through the western and northern sections where artificial rock landscapes predominate. There is also a very beautiful peach tree garden in the northern part. Also in this section of the garden is the Taihu stone, a rock of bizarre shape, six feet high and said to weigh five tonnes.

I loved the Fisherman's Garden. One of the smallest in Suzhou, but also one of the most romantic. Passing through a rather drab entrance gate there was no hint of the beauty that lay hidden behind it. The aim of the early gardeners was to present a pattern of ever-changing landscapes, and this has been achieved to perfection. The winding path constantly alters direction, and so at every corner a new view is presented to surprise and delight the visitor.

Our visit to Suzhou was all too short. I would love to return there one day, but I don't suppose the opportunity will arise.

We were now well into May and already at 8.00 am. the weather was extremely hot. Following a hurried breakfast we were taken by coach to the railway station. Amidst the swarms of slant-eyed humanity and after much pushing and shoving we boarded the soft-seat carriage for Shanghai, one of the largest cities in the world, a bustling dynamic inland port with a population of nearly twelve million. A banking and commercial centre and the largest seaport in China, it is also known as an El Dorado for adventurers and opportunists and for its many bars and the prostitution district; and is an excellent place for browsing around shops. The stores along Nanjing Road in the downtown area have the most abundant, and modern supply of goods in China. Not that Ruth and I care much for city shopping.

For two hours we clickety-clicked at a steady 40/50 kilometres an hour through the intensity cultivated area of the Yangtze delta. The rich alluvial soil which year after year yields fantastic crops bringing life to millions of people but also death and destruction on a frightening scale in times of flood.

At Shanghai's main railway station we had but a short coach journey to the Swan Cindic Hotel which is situated opposite the main entrance to Hongkou Park, and commands a fabulous view of this famous Park. The hotel is in the north eastern part of Shanghai City, yet only ten minutes walk from the downtown business district. This luxurious 17 storey hotel features 208 spacious air-conditioned rooms and suites, the majority of which overlook the gardens where tinkling fountains, softly rustling leaves and lush greenery create a relaxing setting for guests.

Later that same afternoon Ruth and I had time to browse through Shanghai Friendship Store. Six stories high it is the largest in the country catering to foreign visitors. On display were beautiful silk garments, handmade carpets, brightly coloured dresses, smart city suits, cameras, TV's, videos, electrical goods, jade carvings and native products from far flung provinces. To the foreign tourist these items looked ridiculously cheap, mainly being snapped up by Japanese visitors armed with handfuls of money. The Chinese currency is called renminbi (peoples money; renmin=people, bi=money) The basic unit is the yuan. One yuan is divided into 10 jiao or 100 fen. All denominations are issued as bank notes; 1, 2, 5 and 10 yuan notes 1, 2, 5 jiao notes, and finally 1, 2 and 5 fen notes. Whilst we had an ample supply of notes we purchased very little except for an additional suitcase for the equivalent of £11 a third of the price a similar case would have cost us back in England. The Chinese people as a rule are tactful, friendly and co-operative but their customs are so different from those of foreigners, especially Europeans, that some effort at patience and understanding is necessary on both sides. Even in the Friendship Store few of the shop assistants spoke English, it takes a certain amount of mime, hand gestures and patience to overcome the language barrier. I also took note of the fact that the girl behind the till did not use a calculator to add up the total price making full use of the abacus counting frame with lightning movements.

In Shanghai we were certainly given "red carpet" treatment. It seemed to me that our Chinese host always endeavoured to outdo the hospitality of the previous city we had just come from. The banquet laid on for us that evening was just something. After two hours sampling one delicacy after the other, most of the time not being quite sure what we were eating, we were whisked away to a nearby famous theatre. The traditional style singing, brilliant costumes, music from weird string instruments and unbelievable acrobatics was out of this world and a new sight for us foreigners. We eventually crawled into bed in the early hours yet were up again at daybreak in order to get to the nearby park by 6.30 am. It was here amidst the beautiful gardens and green lawns that thousands of Chinese engaged in shadow boxing, that wonderful form of exercise and meditation practised by the masses. Business men, typists, shop assistants, teachers, street cleaners, in fact men and women of all age groups slowly gyrate in perfect unison, mostly in silent, romantic movements to music which issues from speakers discreetly hidden in the trees. Approaching one elderly gentlemen who had just completed his morning exercise session I greeted him in my very limited Chinese and was pleasantly surprised when he smiled and replied in passable English. I was to learn that despite the fact that he was eighty years old, after one hour's work out in the park he spent the rest of the day cleaning and repairing bicycles.

Ruth and I continued our early morning tour of the city by strolling down Nanjing Road, the largest business street in Shanghai. Then onto the Bund. This is the waterfront that borders on the Huangpu River. It was here whilst Ruth was concentrating on capturing the busy and colourful scene on the video camera that we were surrounded by a large crowd of young Chinese students eager to practice their English. They were a very friendly bunch, we were not assailed and at no time did we feel in any danger of losing the camera or our money. I was impressed by the City of Shanghai, people are smartly dressed, there are even a few private motor cars and in the main streets peace reigned as no bikes are allowed between 9.00 am and 6.00 pm and the blowing of vehicle horns is prohibited.

Back again to our hotel we joined the main group once more. Our tour on this day was to include a visit to the Wu Gardens. These fantastic grounds were laid out 400 years ago and we were told took 18 years to construct. We took tea here in the Tea House (or Mid-Lake Pavilion) where our own Queen Elizabeth II had enjoyed a cuppa the previous year.

South of Renmin Road is the old town of Shanghai, often referred to as "Chinatown." Unless one is with a guide it is very easy to get lost in the crooked and narrow alleyways, but somehow we always managed to find a way to one of the large streets that encircle the old town. Countless small stores make it a good place to go shopping if one is that way inclined, and numerous restaurants offer fast foods as well as special dishes. In front of Yuyuan Gardens there is a large square, an old tea house standing there on stilts in the middle of a lake offers cocoa with jasmine tea as its speciality.

Late afternoon our guide arranged for us to visit the silk carpet factory. This is a very labour intensive industry and hundreds work there, mostly women. Some of the larger carpets take three girls six months to complete, laboriously tying each silken thread by hand, working so swiftly it was impossible to follow the movement of their nimble fingers. The training of a skilled worker takes six years, yet at the end of their training wages are but a pittance. This hive of activity I found most interesting and it really made one appreciate the work that goes into producing an oriental masterpiece. At the end of the tour the opportunity was there to purchase a beautiful carpet at a mere fraction of its cost in say Harrods of Knightsbridge.

In Shanghai we were to visit one more large commune, actually inside the City boundaries. Specialising in vegetables for the 'free' market the farmers boasted of growing up to five consecutive crops each year. But, not without rural economic reforms. Yields were boosted by today's technology. The increasing use of fertiliser beyond the organic achievements of 'night soil' was putting a severe strain on supplies of artificial manure. At the party headquarters the farmers generously provided us with a most hearty lunch after which, through our interpreter, a general discussion on farming followed. An interesting day.

A new experience was to visit a Chinese market and Shanghai's was no exception. Early one morning Ruth and I skipped breakfast and made our way down narrow, litter strewn streets and alleyways where we mingled with early risers on their way to work. Bakers working on the pavements had set up a kind of mobile oven, coal and wood provided heat. Three men and a boy had a production line in operation. One man mixed and kneaded the dough, the next rolled, stretched and twisted it, the third man cut it into equal lengths and then it was cooked in a tin of boiling oil. The lad was kept busy wrapping the finished product in a bamboo leaf, handing them over to customers and taking their money. We hadn't yet eaten so we had to try some there and then. Butchers in open fronted shops were putting their meat joints out on display, no attempt was made to protect it from flies or the dust from the streets. They cut the joints up on rough wooden tables, whilst the uncut sides of beef and whole pig carcasses lay out on the concrete floor in the rear of the shop for all to see.

Cleanliness, hygiene and meat inspectors were unknown factors in this part of the world. The market proper occupied a huge open square, packed to absolute capacity with stalls and stands of every description. Vendors weighed produce, such as fungi spices, eels, live ducks and chicken on balancing scales and total up the price on abacuses. Parrots and multi-coloured birds in cages talked and sang, monkeys, hamsters, rabbits and dangerous looking snakes all hoping for new homes before the day was past. Quack dentists, skilful shoe menders and tailors all trying to make a living side by side. For a few yuan one could get immediate repairs to trousers or jackets, buttons sewn on or footwear repaired whilst you wait. Certainly the whole place was alive with enterprise, I even saw one elderly man busy recycling bicycle spokes to sell. There was no shortage of the basic necessities of life, the food stalls were loaded, perhaps by our standards not well presented but the crowds of early morning shoppers were parting freely with their hard-earned cash. At times we were jostled and pushed by the crowd but only because of the sheer mass of humanity. In a quiet corner of the market and nicer by far, were the locust flower garlands which children make and sell. One little girl who approached me was charging one yuan for each. I took one, gave her two yuan and told her to keep the change. She obviously didn't understand my words. She solemnly gave me a second garland. In all my contacts with the Chinese people I was similarly respected in this upright way.

Leaving Shanghai we resumed our journey south, this time by air in a drab two prop military plane, which droned on and on over intensely cultivated paddy fields, buffeted by cross-winds. It was a long flight before landing at Wuhan.

Wuhan, capital of Hubei Province is really three cities in one Wuchang, Hankou and Hanyang. During our stay in this City we enjoyed the luxury of the very modern Qingchuan Hotel which is built on the southern bank of the Yangtze River. Our room in this hotel was on the sixteenth floor. A double glass door opened out to a balcony which gave a marvellous view of the waterway. The next morning we awoke to the sounds of boat horns and hooters from the river traffic. Cargo ships sailing to Hong Kong, Macau, Japan and Southeast Asia, also the passenger ships which sail all the way upstream to Chongching and downstream to Shanghai. This city is different again with beautiful tree lined avenues and it is very noticeable how in this sub-tropical climate these very trees shade the shops and pavements lowering the temperature at street level by some three or four degrees. During our three day stay in Wuhan our hosts decided to show us Huazhong Agricultural College. With 3,200 students and 800 teachers the college farm covers some 550 hectares. Compared to agricultural colleges back in England it made this almost seem like a labour camp. So much of the farm work was done by hand, even to the threshing of rape by the hand flail and the breaking down of a seedbed with a small harrow pulled by a reluctant buffalo!

Our tour of the City included a visit to East Lake. 33sq km in size, with hills, parks and walks along the shore. There are over 70 pavilions, towers and arcades, all of which create the atmosphere of a typical Chinese landscape. We also visited the Provincial Museum which houses the world famous Zhen Houyi bronze chimebells. Yet I must say that after a while one begins to tire of Temples, pagodas, pavilions and innumerable Chinese on bicycles all dressed in the same ill-fitting clothes, but tonight we were due to board the overnight train to Guilin. That in itself turned out to be an unforgettable experience. The Chinese prefer to travel by train and seem to have a knack for turning an overnight trip into something between a pyjama party and a troop train in which everyone shuffles around drinking tea and swapping stories. During this journey my greatest wish was that I had understood enough of the language to engage in conversation with some of the other passengers. Travelling overnight we couldn't pass the time admiring the scenery and sleep was impossible. Still, with Edward in control, our little group of weary travellers got off the train at Guilin's main railway station battered but intact. I was amazed by the fact that a coach was waiting for us even at that early hour. Up to date our hosts were exceeding themselves in their organising abilities. At all times they seemed to know our whereabouts. We were whisked away to the Rougha Hotel for a two night stay, but first on the agenda a bath or a shower was called for, providing water came out of the taps. Then a spot of shut eye.

The highlight of our visit to Guilin was the river cruise. The Li River, like a green ribbon winds its way through numerous weird shaped, limestone hills and it is well-known for its beautiful scenery and gentle waters. The boat we travelled in was a sizeable affair, equipped to carry passengers in relative luxury on the 83 kilometre journey down stream to Yangshou. What was rather unusual was that our boat was pulled by a powerful tug some hundred metres up ahead. One advantage of this method was that because our boat had no engine we got no vibration and we cruised silently. Food and non-alcoholic drinks were available and during the course of this journey we enjoyed an excellent meal, whilst at the same time sampled the scenery of this fantastic land. I was fascinated by the method used on the river to catch fish. Cormorant fishermen poled sampans through the shallows, then their trained birds, sitting silently in rows on the gunwales, dived into the water on command and as often as not surfaced with a fish. It seemed an easy way to earn a living and at the same time get a fish supper. On the bank a farmer in a lampshade hat was ploughing with a water buffalo, knee deep in muddy water turning the big beast carefully at the end of each turn in a paddy the size of a tennis court. Chinese families were labouring in the fields cultivating cabbages, beans, peppers, onions and just about every other vegetable on this extremely fertile land. Little plots which were family heirlooms, hundreds of years old, tilled with elaborate care while across the river terraced paddy-fields climbed to dizzy heights, hugging the contours of the slopes.

The river cruise came to an end all too soon. Getting off the boat at Yangshou we were given an hour to look round this interesting little town before a coach took our group back to Guilin.

Next day was spent sight seeing in the city before taking an evening flight to Guangzhou (known as Canton by Westerners). This sub-tropical city through which the Pearl river meanders on its way to the South China Sea enjoys a mild climate and abundant rainfall and remains luxuriantly green all year round. On our coach tour of the City I noticed that most of the streets were lined with evergreen and flowering trees. One of the great advantages of this tree cover is that the walkways are shaded during the day much reducing heat from the sun. We were accommodated at the Swan Hotel. In my book the best so far. The standard of service was first rate, equal to most of the best European Hotels. Much of our time in Canton was "free time," so Ruth and I took the opportunity to walk the water front capturing the scene on our video. Often we had an audience of young Chinese students engaging us in conversation with the aim of improving their passable English and obtaining some knowledge of Western countries. They were at all times very polite and at no time did we feel threatened.

The time had arrived for us to leave mainland China. Yet another train journey was in the offing. Our group were becoming seasoned travellers, quite adept at pushing and shoving our way through crowds, although I must say we had a certain advantage with our Edward marching boldly in front with his Union Jack held aloft and issuing commands in Mandarin to any Chinaman barring his path. He seemed to excel in showing his authority.

We took the train from Guangzhou to the Kowloon Peninsula in the early morning, passing through highly cultivated rice and wheat fields but even in this area tractors and other mechanical aids were few and far between. Man power and water buffalo seemed to be the power units.

The train passed Shenzhen station then slowed to a stop at the border, a 16 foot high fence guarded largely by the Gurka Brigade, Nepalese troops trained in Britain. This dividing line between China and the New Territories was completed in 1980 when illegal entries were exceeding 150,000 a year. Since our group was the only English and with all our papers in order we had no problems, but some of the Chinese caused a stir with much gesturing and arm waving between themselves and the guards. They all seemed to get very excited over pieces of paper especially if lacking a vital signature. A few unlucky ones were barred from entry but in the main all was well and we continued our train journey to reach our destination, Kowloon where we transferred to the Marco Polo Hotel for a three nights stay. We had left behind the communist system where big brother is always watching you, and travel, especially to other countries is restricted. This was very much a different world.

In the heart of Kowloon scores of tourists laden with shopping bags trudged down the main streets, smart ladies dressed in the latest fashions window shopped and no doubt purchased even more expensive clothes and jewellery. Red double-decker buses weaved through dense traffic, Rolls-Royce, Mercedes, BMW's greatly outnumbered Fords and every third vehicle was a taxi cab. The shops were stuffed with merchandise from all corners of the world, restaurants, coffee shops and food stalls competed for customers and neon lights flashed Chinese advertising symbols all night long. Tailors will make you a suit in a day. In fact in Nathan road alone you will find enough tailors to clothe half the world! Anything to take your money by fair means or foul On a visit to the bank I proffered a hundred pounds for exchange. As the young clerk quickly processed the transaction, he asked me a question. "How long are you in Hong Kong, sir?" "Three days" I replied, rather surprised that he had time to make conversation.

"You are not changing enough for three days" he declared. "How about a thousand pounds? That may last you." Luckily I didn't have that sum on me, but he was quite right, a hundred pounds doesn't go far, especially if you spend time at the Sha Tin Racecourse where the affluent win or lose millions of dollars in an afternoon.

An interesting hour was spent by Ruth and me on the harbour cruise, although I must say there was not much clear water for our boat to negotiate a course. The harbour buzzed with barges, junks and sampans, many of the former permanently moored, the home of many families who live out their lives on the water. In the background white skyscrapers rise out of the green hills beyond, and all around the city workers wrestle with pneumatic drills, demolishing the old to make way for the new. Hong Kong is a place that thrives on work.

For the price of a phone call one can cross on the Star ferry to Victoria on Hong Kong Island. It was a unanimous decision to make this short trip, but as soon as we got off the boat we were accosted by the rickshaw men. Both the two wheeled passenger vehicle, pulled by one man and the similar variety with three wheels, propelled by a man pedalling on a tricycle. Ruth and I viewed Hong Kong by the latter method. A very leisurely ride for a few dollars. We were making our £100 go a long way. I knew it would last out if we kept clear of the racecourse and the casino. We wished it had been possible to extend our stay at the Marco Polo, but our money was running low. On the fourth day we transferred to the airport in time to connect with British Caledonian flight no BA7381 departing for London at 9.30 pm.

On lift-off from Hong Kong's International Airport, as the white skyscrapers were left behind it crossed my mind, with 1997 fast approaching-will the goose continue to lay such golden eggs for its new rulers?

During the last few weeks Ruth and I had travelled thousands of miles through China, by plane, train, coach, rickshaw and on our own two feet. A very rewarding experience, seeing how the other half live. On reflection I much prefer our method of farming, but then it's what you have been brought up to expect I presume. As far as the Chinese peasants are concerned they have never known any other way to farm.

Alaska Bound

June 6th 1994.
D.Day plus 50 years. What a memorial day to start a holiday.

On this particular adventure we intended to visit Alaska, America's 49th state which was purchased from the Russians in 1867 for about £1,450,000. At the time there had been a storm of indignation. Nothing could be more foolish, the critics said, than to pay good gold for a mass of useless glaciers and frozen waste, as the country was thought to be. But since then this icebox in the North American continent has proved to be a treasure chest. But before we arrived there, we had a few pleasant diversions planned which I will briefly describe.

Mrs George Krohn, our kind-hearted neighbour, offered to drive Ruth and me to Heathrow. She is a skilled driver and in light traffic it took less than one hour to speed up the M4 in her BMW. Dropping us off at Terminal 3, we were there by 11.00 am, in ample time for our flight with Air Canada at 3.15 pm. Flight number 859 direct to Winnipeg, Manitoba's provincial capital. Time spent in the departure lounge soon goes by, a four hour wait left me with time to read the Daily Telegraph and almost complete the crossword, which I seldom have time for. I can always amuse myself too, by 'people watching'. I find it fascinating to watch all the many nationals in their diverse choice of clothes, many clearly mystified by the direction signs in English and at the same time keeping tags on vagrant children.

Our flight was ten minutes late on take-off. We left Heathrow in dense cloud cover, but this soon gave way to perfect weather conditions as we passed over the Lake District. At this point a thought crossed my mind of my step-son Bill Fiddler and his family striving to make a living on his tiny patch of Lancashire. Still climbing, the big jet loaded to capacity, crossed the lowlands of Scotland before changing course to swing out over the Outer Hebrides. We were already enjoying the first in-flight meal as we crossed Iceland heading west at six hundred miles per hour and at a height of 39,000 feet. Another hour and we were over Greenland, a mountainous land of ice and snow. Five hours into our flight and we had reached the rugged, ice-locked shores of north-east Canada. Glancing back at the rows of seats I noticed yet another meal was on its way. Having just altered our time pieces, I couldn't figure out which meal this was, the only thing I was sure about was that I wasn't hungry. Two hours later the plane began to lose height in the steady decent to our scheduled landing at Winnipeg airport. We had booked accommodation for a few nights in the City with every intention of exploring the area before continuing our journey to Saskatoon.

Now I am not a racing man, but our visit to Winnipeg clashed with the big meeting of the year. So, we went to the horse races, travelling there is style on the 'Racetrack Express'. Situated on the Assiniboia Downs at the junction of the Perimeter Highway 100 and the Trans-Canada Highway 1. The track is a mere 20 minutes from downtown Winnipeg. Perhaps not quite as up market as Newbury's Course, nevertheless it is great fun and has a rodeo atmosphere. Jockeys in colourful silks guide turf pounding thoroughbreds to record-breaking performances. I studied form in the paddock although I knew neither horse nor their riders, I was sure I could pick a likely winner. I followed this procedure for the first three races, but the horses I put my money on came nowhere. Next I tried a new tactic betting heavily on the favourite at 2 to 1. It led the field all the way, but lapsed in the last few furlongs. Of course there are the 'Ask Me Booths' with friendly attendants who will gladly answer all your questions and hand out brochures free of charge on 'How To Play The Horses'. But I decided to go it alone. One more race to go -the 'big' one- there was a rank outsider running at 50 to 1, just for a laugh I put 10 dollars on him to win, simply because I liked its name. 'Lucky for Some'. It won by three lengths. I'd well covered my previous losses!

On the next leg of our Trans-Canada journey we flew to Saskatoon, high above the flat, patchwork fields of grain and summer fallow in less than two hours. Yet in the early days of this century my father had walked those six hundred miles in two months on the trail, so much for modern day travel. We landed at Saskatoon airport out of a cloudless sky, awaiting our arrival were my cousins Merv and Jean. What a welcome we received and what a lovely feeling it is to have relatives waiting to greet you at every stop-over. They took us to their town apartment before taking us next day on the 250 mile drive north to La Ronge. On this journey we stopped briefly at a MacDonald's where we found that pensioners got free coffee, but first you had to buy a Big Mac. There has got to be a catch in every give-away. Next stop Eagle Point. Shopping for two weeks supplies which we would be taking with us on the boat to Houghton Island. Gas, food, drink etc., once we got out to the island we had to be sufficient in everyday requirements. One cannot slip down to the corner shop because one has run out of bread or forgotten the matches.

On this crossing the waters of the lake were reasonably calm, just a few white horses out in open water we cruised at a steady 20 knots on the forty-five minute journey to Houghton Island.

What a proud day it must have been for my first cousin, Harry when his life's work was officially recognised by the provincial government.

> In Appreciation.
> Houghton Island is named after Henry James 'Harry' Houghton.
> Latitude 55 degrees 10'00"
> Longitude 104 degrees 54'00"
> Adopted July 10th 1984
> Certified by the Saskatchewan Geographic Names Board.

Although Canada's northern bush is disconcertingly monotonous to many people I find it interesting, an adventure land. Ruth and I just love the peace and quiet, the solitude and the wild beauty of this vast empty land. Once we had settled down on the island, top priority for Ruth and me was to get close up views on our video camera of the eagles. For the first time in years they had built their nest on the island. The image of an eagle arouses many different emotions in people. To many, a sense of power and grandeur. Something that in 1782 inspired the people of the United States to adopt this bird as their national symbol. When you see it perched motionless on a dead branch, on the tallest tree in the area, its head glistening pearly white in the sun, or soaring gracefully in a light breeze, this magnificent bird is truly awe inspiring. Powerful yellow feet and sharp black talons are the tools a Bald Eagle uses to secure its prey. The wings of the bird are six to seven feet from tip to tip when fully stretched. A day or two later as we sailed around the island in Merv's boat we watched and marvelled at the ability of this bird to soar higher and higher, circling into the crisp blue summer sky on a column of rising air. Suddenly, with no warning of any kind, it hurled itself at full speed on to a school of fish, scooped one out of the water and flew back to its nest

Fishing in Pickerole Bay. Lac La Ronge

Merv guts the day's catch on our return to Houghton Island

with its solitary, hungry youngster.

Another beautiful day. After a delicious breakfast of pancakes and maple syrup, followed by fresh fruit, we planned to walk the new trail to the northern end of the island, two miles through dense bush. We took with us axes and bushman saws to clear the winter fall of trees across the path and tied red tape on pathside trees to blaze the trail. It was only the previous year that the north of the island had been fully explored and the southern half still awaits the feet of man.

The following morning, once again, the sun shone out of a cloudless sky, and a strong breeze blew from the west. Luckily not too strong to prevent our planned trip to Pickerole Bay for a day's fishing. Merv, Jean, Ruth and I left the dock at 9.30 am fully equipped with four rods, lines, ox heart bait and all necessary provisions for a day on the lake. On the way we called at a depot on another island where it was possible to refuel the boat and also most important obtain an angling licence for Ruth and myself. As visitors to the country we should have paid 30 dollars each, which would have covered us for a year's fishing. However, Merv suggested we posed as Senior Canadian Citizens and adopt his address in Saskatoon. Merv wrote down his address and told the attendant that his cousin 'didn't hear to good' and there was no point talking to him. For one thing Merv didn't want the man to hear my Berkshire accent, a dead give away. This innocent deception saved me 40 dollars! I had no qualms really after all the licence was for a year and I only required a few days cover. Safely across the lake and in possession of an angling licence, once in the shelter of the bay we lost no time in casting out our lines. Pickerole or Walleye are only present in this bay during June, they come to feed, having spawned on the other side of the lake. Typical of my wife, she caught the first fish, quite a decent size one I should add, but her next catch was a monster. She had quite a fight on her hands to bring it in. After two hours of hectic excitement we had reached our combined quota for the day which was twenty fish. We packed up and turned for our island home. Back once more Merv gutted our catch at the dockside. Barbecued fish for supper-Yummy-and the deep freeze was well stocked too!

Every day the summer sun shone out of a cloudless sky, yet despite this fact I forecast rain was on its way. "What makes you say that, seldom rains up here this time of year" Merv said with some surprise. I hadn't heard rain was forecast on the radio I didn't have to, there had been a distinct halo around the moon the night before. By morning the sky was full of 'mare's-tails'-high feathery cirrus clouds that looked like hen scratchings. Weather watchers like myself, take many of their clues from the sky. Mare's-tails, or cirrus clouds, are made of ice crystals and precede a large, slow-moving warm front. These ice crystals, found in high-level clouds can cause halos around the sun or moon and are handy indicators of bad weather to come. Cirrus clouds arrive several hours to a day before a storm and are followed by altocumulus clouds, which often look like a flock of small fluffy lambs but are often called 'mackerel scales', Finally, these are followed by grey rain clouds. Caution, these weather signs are not always accurate, but after six decades of forecasting I trust these methods as much as the BBC weather man! Well, it did rain, also became much cooler. cold enough for Merv to light the "Old Timer," his wood burning stove and cook a North American breakfast. Pancakes, made from 'Coyote' flour from Alberta, a stack each with crispy bacon. Sets one up for the day, there's no doubt about that. Later the weather cleared so we took out the big boat sailing over to 'Hunter's Bay' to cast for 'Jack' fish. These big fellows are a striking fish and provide excellent sport. Unfortunately they didn't strike well for us and our catch was mediocre.

The next day the weather turned angry, forcing us to stay put in the comfort of our log cabin. An unseasonal gale came roaring in from the east, whipping up huge waves on the lake.

The boat, moored at the dock, tugged and pulled on the ropes. A radio message from friends on a nearby island informed us that their boat had been sunk. We just hoped that our boat didn't suffer the same fate, because it was our only means of leaving the island and we were due to leave for the mainland at 7.00 am the next morning, as we had a flight booked from Saskatoon airport on the Wednesday. The storm lasted all that day and through the following night, but by morning it had eased. It was decided to attempt the crossing back to La Ronge by taking a longer, seldom used route finding shelter behind other islands. Slowing the boat to a crawl in what was obviously shallow water, Merv placed me up front on the lookout for any rocks showing close to the surface. Unfortunately I saw the danger too late, with a resounding bang the boat struck the reef. "Good grief those rocks are close to the surface, didn't you see them Bert?" If the water comes in Ruth, put this rubber cover over the hole and sit on it." Luckily our contact with rocks had not ripped the bottom out and without further mishap we made it to port in 2 hours 20 minutes. Safely back on the mainland we transferred our luggage to their large car which had been parked nearby. Then we were off on the 250 mile journey to Saskatoon. The maximum speed limit allowed on this particular road is 100 kilometres per hour. Merv, anxious to make up lost time, set cruise control at 110 k/ph, then still not satisfied hiked it up to 120. No speed cops in these northern parts, says Merv with a laugh. The words were hardly out of his mouth when, blue lights flashing, a patrol car pulled us in. Two big RCMP got out and casually strolled over to our vehicle looking very smart in their uniforms and knee-length black leather boots, complete with ominous side arms on their hips. "Our radar tracked your speed at 122k's per hour sir, I'm afraid I must give you an on the spot speeding ticket, you were well over the limit". It cost Merv 70 dollars plus 1 dollar for every unit of speed over the hundred, plus another 10 dollars administration fee, total 102 dollars about £50. An unnecessary expensive journey, especially as when we did get to the airport we had a three hour wait for our plane!

We flew over the Rocky Mountains to Vancouver, stayed the night at a posh hotel then on the next day embarked on the ferry boat 'Queen of Nanaimo'. Our destination, Otter Bay, Pender Island. Now if I had been asked a month or so before the whereabouts of the Gulf Islands, I would have been at a loss to place them on the world map. However, with relatives living in this beautiful part of the globe I am now just that little bit more knowledgeable.

Snuggled against the southeast of Vancouver Island the Gulf Islands lie sheltered from the rain and blustery winds that blow from the Pacific. Some two hundred of these enchanting islands and islets are clustered on the leeward side of Vancouver Island. Most of these islands are uninhabited and accessible only by boat, the populated islands Saltspring, Galiano, Mayne, Suturna, North and South Pender- are linked with Vancouver Island and the mainland by a fleet of government operated car and passenger ferries. We hadn't seen Ted and Dianne since our Churchill adventure two years previous. They were at the dockside to meet us off the ferry. As to be expected we got a warm welcome and were soon whisked off to their retirement home- Treasure Cottage, a typical Canadian timber house built on a rocky slope with wonderful views over the blue waters of the Georgia Strait. We stayed three weeks on this captivating island which is about the size of the Isle of Wight, yet only has a population of about one thousand people. We spent our time visiting the many fascinating little creeks where we often enjoyed a picnic lunch and then usually I fell asleep in some shaded spot. Ted and Ruth spent hours diligently searching the beach for unusual shaped bits of driftwood washed up by the tide, whilst Dianne looked for rare coloured pebbles which she took back to the cottage to polish with a power-driven sander until they looked like jewels. On one remote beach Ruth took close up video pictures of the rare sea otter, which in the 1980's after heavy persecution was thought to be extinct, but has now made a slight comeback.

June 19th.1994.

At last the day had arrived for the start of the Houghton/Scoles adventure trip to Alaska. It was a beautiful morning approaching mid-summers day when the four of us, taking Ted's car, boarded the ferry for the 30 minute journey from Pender Island dock to Victoria. Once ashore we wasted no time setting off on the 307 mile drive, destination Port Hardy situated on the northern tip of Vancouver Island. Following the highway north of the Campbell River we were to discover the magic of Vancouver Island with its tall forests, uncrowded lakes and beaches. We made brief stops at places with fascinating names like Woss, Nimpkish, Zeballos and Alert Bay. Unfortunately time did not allow us to do much exploring, as it was we ended up arriving at our B&B stop-over very late in the day. Luckily Dianne had had the foresight to book in advance. The cruise ship 'Queen of the North', flagship of B.C. Ferries, was due to sail on the high tide early next morning. Ted's car was left by arrangement at our B&B hosts until our return from Alaska. Slipping quietly out of Port Hardy between Scarlett Point and Pine Island, one has a grand view of the mountains of the coast range on the eastern seaboard. On crossing Queen Charlotte Sound, looking westwards I realised there was no land until the Orient which probably accounted for the vicious swells born of storms hundreds of miles away. This made for a very rough crossing until gaining the shelter of the Inner Passage with its protection of hundreds of off shore islands. Travelling by ferry as opposed to a cruise liner, one can disembark at ports on the way, spend a day or two ashore and then catch the next ferry going north.

Our itinerary allowed for stop-overs at Prince Rupert and Juneau. We spent two nights in Prince Rupert, June 21st and 22nd, staying at the Aleeda Motel. 55 dollars per couple per night, senior citizens rate. As a matter of passing interest, Ruth and I celebrated under a magnificent display of the Northern Lights, the fifteenth anniversary of my marriage proposal. How romantic!

It was during our brief stay in Prince Rupert that we decided to join the locals at their annual fete and I got called in to dance with the Indians. Much to the amusement of the onlookers, I was soon doing the blanket dance as well as the professionals.

June 23rd at 8.30 am.
We sailed from Prince Rupert on the good ship 'Malaspina'. Towards nightfall crossing the Alaska/Canadian border sailing northwards up the Inner Passage. At this point in time much to the amusement of our better halves Ted and I agreed to take turns in 'ordering' the next day's weather, both claiming that we had supernatural powers to do so. In my case, more by luck than judgement, I was surprisingly successful. I claimed to have ordered a wet day as we approached Ketchikan, Alaska's southernmost major city. Sure enough as we breakfast on muffins and bacon, the rain cascaded down making for almost nil visibility with no dividing line between sea and sky. It was no great forecast really, Ketchikan has a mild, wet climate and receives over 400 centimetres of precipitation a year. "Your turn tomorrow Ted, see what you can do". " I'm going to order ten hours of sunshine, I've had enough of this, you can stuff your English weather", said Ted with a wry grin. It was on this part of our cruise that Ruth, looking out on our port side caused great excitement amongst our fellow passengers, by getting the first sighting of Humpback whales as they played in the water amusing everyone with their tail-flipping act. It certainly got cameras and videos working overtime! At noon we glided

quietly into the Gastineau Channel and docked at Juneau, Alaska's third largest city. and incidentally the state capital. Juneau, with 30,000 residents can only be reached by air or sea, as there are no roads to the place, which gives it a certain amount of isolation from the rest of America. Whilst in the area we took the opportunity to visit the Mendenhall Glacier, a mighty river of ice two miles across at the mouth. It is one of the few glaciers in Alaska that can be reached with ease. Out of Juneau we switched to an American ferry sailing northwards on the last leg of our journey by water.

Destination Skagway, the 'Gateway to the Yukon'. This place I am told owes its birth to the Gold Rush of 1898, but today gold counts but little. It's the dollars in the tourist wallets that the locals extract by whatever means possible both legal or illegal. We had hotel rooms booked in town, for a three day stay, having travelled so far we planned to look the place over. Skagway, with its Wild West character and frontier history, is the most popular stop on Alaska cruises. There was a carnival on whilst we were there with a parade of Royal Canadian Mounted Police from across the border, Boy Scouts and a drive past of old motor vehicles, motor cycles and fire engines. Brazen as ever I mounted the VIP stand and took the salute with the other dignitaries. That evening, our first in town, we made our way to the casino to test our skill, or lack of it, playing black jack with the locals. Not with real money thank goodness! It is a little known fact that Alaska is the only state in the Union where gambling is prohibited. With the purchase of an entrance ticket, one is given 1000 dollars of 'monopoly-like' money, you either made a million or go bust! Of course Ted and I couldn't visit Skagway without downing a beer or two in the disreputable Red Onion saloon. During the gold rush days the Red Onion saloon was Skagway's most exclusive bordello and opened for business in 1898 serving intoxicating drinks on the first floor while the upper floor satisfied more than the prospector's thirst.

Second day in town: Today was Ted's day for the weather and to be quite truthful up to now he hadn't made much of a job of it. We rose at 7.00 am to a grey overcast morning with a heavy drizzle, but he promised that on the weather front, things would get better and that we would be enjoying sunshine by noon. We had simply risen too early!

No trip to Alaska is complete without an adventure over the White Pass and back into Canada and the Yukon on what is arguably 'The Scenic Railway of the World'. The adventure begins at Skagway, where you board a vintage parlour car, painted sparkling emerald green and with much polished brass. It is straight out of the 1890's. Route map in hand we settled into comfortable seats and peered out through the big, wide windows. Suddenly we were on our way and soon passing the town cemetery where at least one of the town's notorious citizens rests in peace. Soapy Smith, con-man supreme of the gold rush days who was finally killed in a gun battle by a disgruntled punter. Equipped with a powerful diesel engine that easily handles the grade, the train skirts the rushing torrents of the Skagway River, gaining elevation through a narrow box canyon. Then up, up grey rock cliffs that rise nearly perpendicular from the valley floor. Next moment we were out in the open, crawling along the shoulder of a mountain. A wooden trestle bridge spans a deep gorge into a seemingly insurmountable mountain wall. Suddenly the train disappears into a tunnel, emerging ten minutes later alongside visible remains of the infamous Trail of '98 worn into the rock by the feet of thousands of gold crazed stampeders and the hooves of the weary pack animals. The train forged steadily upwards until we reached the snow-covered summit of White Pass at 2,865 fcct. Hcrc crossing the border we passed into the Canadian Yukon. At this point the would-be millionaires of the gold rush days still had over 500 miles to fight their way through inhospitable mountain country, but we decided to turn back catching the next returning train to Skagway, the ferry and the long, long journey to Pender Island and finally the green fields of England.

However, before we got back to Port Hardy an incident occurred which I think is worth recording:-

Summary of a Conversation with a Canadian Schoolboy.

July 1st 1994

Ruth and I were in Prince Rupert B.C. on the return journey from Skagway, Alaska, accompanied by my cousin Dianne and her husband Ted Scoles. In aid of various charities, the Lions Club were running a fete set out in beautiful Cow Down Park which lays along the wind sheltered shoreline of the Inner Passage. We chose to join the crowds of people, family groups, teenagers and the elderly decked out in bright summer clothes, as they wandered around the stalls and side shows. Ted and Dianne had disappeared amongst the crowd, Ruth, no doubt busy elsewhere with her video camera. I was engrossed in watching a native carving small souvenir totem poles, when a young lad of about 10 years of age standing nearby looked up to me and said, "Clever isn't he?" The boy had a mischievous, yet friendly face. I took to him from the start.

"What's your name?" I asked.

"Robert, Robert Webster."

"How old are you then?"

" I'm 10 nearly 11."

"Oh, do you live in Prince Rupert?" I asked.

"Sure"

He mentioned the name of a street, but it didn't mean anything to me.

"Do you go to school here in the city?"

"Yep."

"Do you like school?"

"Nope not much."

"What do you like doing?"

"Fishing, swimming, just mucking around."

With that I moved on and Robert followed. We continued a running flow of conversation.

"Where do you come from then?" he enquired. His curiosity no doubt aroused by my strange Berkshire accent.

"England," I replied.

"Coo, that's a long way away, we learn English History at school, all about the Queen and that."

"Oh, do you." I was mildly surprised, but after all we were in British Columbia, perhaps the most English part of Canada.

The conversation continued to flow as we strolled from stall to stall.

"Do you see the Queen much?" Robert asked eagerly.

"Oh, yes now and again." I replied modestly and at the same time trying hard to recall how often 'now and again' really was. Giving it some thought I realised that the last time I had seen her Majesty was some eight years ago at the Badminton Horse Trials, and the time before that, around 1980 when she came to Newbury on the 500th anniversary, celebrating the founding of St. Bartholomew's Comprehensive School. "You see," I continued rather boastfully, "Windsor Castle is just up the road from where I live, maybe 30 miles or so, and Buckingham Palace about 50 miles. By distances in Canada, that makes the Queen and I almost next-door neighbours." Robert was quiet for a while, no doubt digesting this information. But not for long!

"What she got two places for?"

"Well, one's a town house and the other is a country retreat, somewhere to go at the week-end when she is not working."

"What work does she do then?"

"Oh, lots of writing, signing important documents, opening new buildings, launching new ships, all sorts, she is a very busy lady. 'Sides living in Town is handy for shopping too. 'Course the Queen never takes any money with her when she shops, all put on the account, then Prince Philip pays I expect."

"Hmm, no wonder she is rich if she never pays for anything."

Sound logic on Robert's part, I thought.

"I've seen pictures of the Palace on the telly, big high fence all round, with lots of people looking through the iron bars all day long."

"Yes," I replied, "like monkeys at a zoo, only difference is they are on the outside looking in, 'stead of on the inside looking out!"

"Then there's the guards marching up and down with rifles and fixed bayonets then they stop and stand in front of little boxes. What they got those boxes for anyway?"

"They stand in them when it rains, keeps their bearskin hats dry I suppose."

"What's it matter if their hats get wet?" "The bears don't worry about it raining, I've seen bears jump into the river to catch salmon on the salmon runs. They splash in and grab a big salmon, get their fur wet through, don't trouble a bit."

"Well, I don't know Robert, you think of a better answer."

Questions, questions, it was getting a bit much, but then I realised Robert was anxious to make the most of the opportunity to learn more about England and the Royal Family. So I kept quiet patiently resigning myself to the next question. I didn't have long to wait.

"What does the Queen and Prince Philip do at their country house?"

"Well, for one thing you can always tell when the Queen is in residence, her flag, the Royal Standard flutters proudly in the breeze above the battlements of the castle. They probably have a restful week-end after the bustle of the city. She wouldn't have to do any housework, cook, or wash clothes of course. She's got lots of servants to do that. Walk the gardens, maybe go for a ride with Prince Philip around Windsor Great Park in a Landau."

"What's a Landau?"

I realised I'd get that question as soon as I said the word, but it was too late to retract.

"It's a four-wheeled horse-drawn carriage with two folding hoods, pulled by four matching horses-four in hand. One holds the reins of all four horses in one hand, whilst at the same time being in complete control, very skilful really. Then in the season Prince Philip may well join a shooting party and go out to shoot pheasants on the estate. The Queen joins the party sometimes, but she doesn't shoot, she just stands behind the line of guns to watch proceedings. The game keeper and his assistants rear lots of pheasants during spring and summer, then when the birds are fully grown, walk in line with dogs and beaters through the coverts driving the birds over the waiting guns." I could see that Robert was giving this activity some deep thought.

"Why don't they just shoot them on the ground?" He asked. I had to smile to myself.

"That wouldn't be fair now would it? Got to give them a sporting chance, although some pheasants refuse to fly, they run and hide in the undergrowth, especially the wily old cock birds."

"So would I if a lot of men with guns were shooting at me, they are a bloodthirsty lot if you ask me, more like a lot of Red Indians."

"Look, they are going to cut the cake," says an excited Robert pointing to a crowd of people gathered in front of a long trestle table behind which stood two courtly gentlemen and a rather elegant lady in a bright summer dress. I was only too glad to drop our discussion on the Royal Family, it had become tedious. Apparently to celebrate Canada Day two huge cakes each a metre square were going to be cut and distributed to the crowd. "Com'on," says Robert, "let's join the queue before it's all gone." The cakes were beautifully decorated with the maple leaf flag of Canada and words in coloured icing that I couldn't read since the writing was upside down from where I was standing. Two chefs were cutting the cakes into little squares whilst two more ladies handed out each piece on a paper serviette. Robert soon pushed his way to the front of the queue, I wasn't far behind him.

We sat back from the crowd on the lush, green grass of the park, quite content to enjoy this free hand-out.

"Here, how come you got two squares of cake?" I enquired.

"Piece for me and one for my young brother," he replied.

"How old is he then?"

"Six."

"But he's not here is he?"

"No so I'm going to eat it for him," said Robert with a crafty grin.

"Haven't you got a brother?"

"No, but I've got a sister."

"Well queue up again, say you forgot your sister wanted a slice of cake. I would."

"I know you would, but I don't think I'll bother, there is a lot of other people who want their share."

After this episode we wandered on. Next a stall selling raffle tickets in aid of yet another charity. Two glamorous blondes waved booklets. Lucky numbers, all in aid of a good cause, only a dollar each. First prize 1000 dollars plus lots of smaller prizes, draw at 2 o'clock at the Band Stand.

"Let's have a bash." I said.

"I got no money," says Robert looking crestfallen.

"Never mind, I'll buy you a ticket, but look, if I do and you win, you will have to share the prize money with me."

"OK, I'll go along with that, but what if you win, you going to share with me?"

"Well that's hardly fair if I buy the tickets is it?" I capitulated.

"All right Robert, you win, we'll make a deal on that arrangement." We seriously shook hands making it legal.

"What you going to buy with your money Robert?"

He looked up at the sky, pulled a face before replying.

"A mountain bike like my friend has got, what you going to buy?"

"I haven't decided yet I'll make that decision if my number comes up."

It goes without saying that when the draw was made at 2.00 pm we didn't draw the lucky number.

Robert pulled my arm. "Come on, I can smell the hot dog stand and I'm hungry."

"But you have only just eaten two slices of cake." I protested.

"And you haven't got any money either."

"No, but you have," he said cheerfully.

Another long queue, but the appetising smell sustained us whilst we waited patiently. We inched forward slowly, it was almost our turn to be served when the man said. "Sorry folks, that's the last, no more bread rolls, had 400 when I started this morning." Crestfallen we turned away, but Robert wasn't one to be beaten easily.

"Over there look, the popcorn lady, d'you like popcorn?"

"Sure." (That's Canadian for yes)

"Hurry up then or they will be sold out too."

For the next half hour we wandered from stall to stall, from one amusement to the next munching popcorn noisily from a large plastic container, a young Canadian schoolboy and a retired English farmer. A very odd combination one would agree, but we did have one thing in common-we both liked popcorn!!

Death Valley and Grand Canyon Country

When my first son was born in 1947 everyone told me that I was a lucky man. I'd got a successor for my farming enterprise, a son to continue in my footsteps when I was gone. Of course things didn't work out like that, they seldom do. Michael wisely had other ideas about what to do with his life. From an early age Michael had mastered most farm jobs, but not with great enthusiasm, mainly I suspect from parental pressure! Blessed with a brilliant mathematical mind it was obvious he was not cut out to "plough the fields and scatter". He easily won a place at university, gained his degree and took up work in the computer industry. Today he is a Senior Systems Engineer for Intel Corporation (UK) Ltd. In 1982 he was transferred to Los Angeles for a couple of years to work on computerising the British telephone system. It was at this moment in time that he suggested Ruth and I flew out to L.A for a holiday, which I am glad to say we took him up on. Michael, his wife Gina and Daniel, my eldest grandson were at the time living in an attractive condominium in a secluded part of the city one mile inland from Redonda Beach, that beautiful stretch of golden sand that is today famous for sun-tanned lifeguards and scantily clad girls in the Baywatch TV series. This was a marvellous opportunity to take a cheap holiday in the renowned Californian sun. Michael suggested a date to coincide with his annual vacation. "One thing I want to do is explore Death Valley" stated Michael over the telephone one evening. Death Valley is undeniable desert, lying as it does in Southern California between the high, cold Great Basin Desert to the north and the warmer Mojave Desert to the south. It is a blistered land of searing sun with summertime temperatures which often surpass 120 degrees Fahrenheit in the shade. Most of the valley is saltpan, a vast accumulation of salts that covers more than 200 square miles upon which no life can grow. I can think of more exciting places to take a holiday but I must admit it proved to be an experience of a life-time and one that I wouldn't wish to miss.

The direct flight from Heathrow to L.A was uneventful. By now Ruth and I had become seasoned travellers. Michael met us at the airport, piled our luggage in his car and drove with confidence through rush-hour traffic back to his apartment, where Gina had prepared an appetising meal which hopefully would be followed by a good nights sleep. Four o'clock in the morning, my time clock adrift, I listened to rain pouring down outside. We had come to California for it's legendary sunshine. How dare it rain on our first night. Later at breakfast I said to Mike and Gina, "Quite a storm last night, I thought we had left the rain back in England" Michael looked surprised, "It didn't rain Dad, that was the automatic watering system you heard sprinkling the flowers and shrubs in the communal gardens".

Two days later all five of us squeezed into Michael's car and headed east into the Mojave Desert. Los Angeles lies in a basin between the San Gabriel Mountains and the Pacific Coast and is frequently obscured by fog. To say that it is a busy place is an understatement, it's like a human ant hill, day or night it never stops. From Michael's apartment to finally clear the city is a drive of almost sixty miles. The displeasing roadside posters get less and less, the eight lane highway continues to drop a lane, the police cars become less obvious and the drive-in restaurants peter out. By now just a single macadam strip disappears over the horizon with nothing but dust blown sand and cottontop cactus on either side. Occasionally a monstrous lorry appears out of the heat haze, its driver blasts away on the huge silver double horn as it passes, which I suppose is some form of greeting or just a warning to get out of the way. We stopped overnight in a motel at Barstow. Next day with cruise control set at 80k per hour, we pressed on across the flat, featureless plain until the road, such as it is swings north following the Amargosa River between the Confidence Hills and the Black Mountains. I had no idea what to expect in this the apparent dead world of Death Valley. My first surprise was the saltpan, a lake of dried salt as far as the eye could see. Glassy heat waves danced above harsh, white salt, while dust devils twist gracefully across a vast desert floor. What a blessing that we have air-conditioning in the car and plenty of liquid refreshment. Surrounding the salt, huge alluvial fans flow from deep within the mountain canyons, and on the highest peaks the snow gleams, even in this heat. Life does exist in Death Valley, but simply driving through there is not much evidence, mainly because during the heat of the day animals take shelter from the sun. Horned lizards, kangaroo rats, burrowing owl, gecko, the sidewinder and of course that comical looking bird the roadrunner is to name but a few. I was certainly glad we were motorised and not on horseback or even walking. I asked myself, "However did those early prospectors survive in this place, or for that matter the Shoshone Indians who made their homes here?". Two hours later we had reached Badwater minus 282 feet, the lowest elevation in the United States and in contrast from this spot one gets a clear view of Telescope Peak 11,331 feet above sea level just 15 miles away. The next part of our tour took us through the Devil's Golf Course, a most weird place. Death Valley has no outlet to the sea and its streams-often fringed by salt-encrusted banks -are saltier than any ocean. The salts have been carried by water from the rocky highlands surrounding the valley. Another hours drive past Twenty-Mule-Team Canyon and we thankfully pulled into the Visitor Center at Furnace Creek, an oasis in what is reputed to be the hottest and driest place in North America, some say the hottest place in all the world. A place where one can fry an egg on the bonnet of your car in two minutes flat! Here in today's world they cater for the tourist. A motel, smart restaurant, gas station and just about everything else modern man demands. We stayed two nights in this spot, sheltered from the sun by palm trees, relaxing, enjoying the excellent cuisine and dancing in the cool of the evening to a very lively jazz band. Of course we couldn't come to this part of the world without a visit to Walter Scott's castle. Scotty was a gold miner who found gold nuggets in the area, at least he thought they were gold and on the strength of his find, persuaded a rich benefactor to build him a castle in Grapevine Canyon below snow-capped Tin Mountain. The next point of interest for this weary group of travellers was the Ubehebe Crater. The largest of a group of volcanoes in the northern end of Death Valley, a desolate area of shifting sands where the wind sweeps unhindered across the valley, piling sand in ever-changing patterns. Michael set up his camera tripod to take some photos as the sun set over the crater with the multi-colour mountain range in the background. That's my story behind the scenery, a brief description of my experience in this immense, wild land that man has never been able to tame. The days had been oven hot, the nights cold. I was not sorry when we left the valley by the only road west through Mosaic Canyon, up and over the Cottonwood Mountains making for the snow line of Sierra Nevada and the bristlecone pines, those grotesque trees that lay claim to being the oldest in the world.

What a contrast it had been. In one day's travel we had left the oppressive heat of the desert to walk in the snow amongst those interesting old trees high in the mountains.

Stopping overnight in a motel, next day we made for San Francisco, but turned off south before reaching the City. I particularly wanted to survey that vast strip of land that is arguably one of the richest fruit and vegetable growing areas in the world. If you are one of those people that enjoy strawberries, melons and other exotic fruit sent over from the United States 10 to 1 this is where they came from.

We got back to L.A. on Sunday. Michael was due back at work the following day. The next couple of weeks Ruth and I gave the city the once over, visiting many places of interest such as the Universal Studios. Here we took a ride on a fun train which on its journey round the grounds skirts a lake and at one point, unexpectedly a huge shark, jaws agape makes a violent grab at the screaming passengers. It's the model of the shark used in the film Jaws II. The next moment the train is rattling over a rickety, wooden trestle bridge which realistically collapses just as the last carriage passes over. Another day was spent at Disney World. I thought this entertainment was only for the kids, but I was soon to discover that they cater for all age groups. We could have spent a week in the place and still not seen it all. A lot of our time was spent on the beach. As I have said it was only a mile to walk from the family's condominium and Daniel always accompanied us. He loved the golden sands and an additional treat was the giant ice-creams we bought him everyday, two each during some days if the weather was very hot!

"Mike, Ruth and I will have to be making tracks for home soon, we mustn't outstay our welcome." I announced over breakfast one morning. "Oh, you're not going yet, I've got another trip in mind for you both. Whilst you are in this part of the world, you must visit the Grand Canyon. I've got to return to work tomorrow as you know, but I suggest you hire a car and drive out there. It's a fair way from here, a thousand miles or so return trip across the Mojave desert, but once you leave the city proper and hit the dirt, the miles will melt away. If you like I will book you a double room in one of the hotels on the South Rim for a few nights." "I'm game, I'll try anything once." I replied. Two days later, preparations made, Ruth and I were on our latest adventure.

The drive out of L.A. was a nightmare. Three, four lanes of traffic in each direction, innumerable interchanges, road-rage drivers cut us up, they passed on either side, and in my view we were all driving on the wrong side of the road anyway! But once we cleared the city, peace at last. I cruised east on good straight roads at 80k per hour, eating up the miles. We stayed overnight in a 'Best Western', continuing our journey next morning. The scenery was monotonous, a flat, featureless desert of sand, scrub bushes and cacti. On and on, it seemed for hours. "When we do reach this canyon it had better be good." I repeated for the tenth time.

Approaching a mountain range one can see first the foothills then the higher peaks from 20 to 30 miles away, but nearing this vast chasm in the earth's surface, there was no indication of any change in the normal terrain. And then suddenly there it was, I nearly drove over the edge! A chasm 277 miles long and in places 18 miles wide. It is the most awesome and spectacular sight I have ever seen. I cannot even begin to describe it accurately. And, 1 mile below ground level, unseen from where we stood flows the mighty Colorado River. A river 1,400 miles long, which drains nearly 12% of the United States. Weary after our long drive and covered in fine dust-despite the cars air conditioning, I drove alongside this cleft in the earth's surface until reaching Grand Canyon Village where we confirmed our booking at the El Tover Hotel. Next day, refreshed after a swim in the hotel pool, an excellent evening meal, and a good nights sleep, we were raring to get going, and see at close hand this canyon which is truly one of the spectacular sights on the planet. Initially we did it the easy way. A flight in a modern Bell Jet Helicopter, a flight of just 65 minutes duration which took us well below the rim of the Canyon. After flying over a peaceful pine forest suddenly, dramatically, the ground fell away beneath us. What a thrill as we first encounter the Grand Canyon from the best seat in the house. My written word cannot describe the excitement as our pilot swooped low over the raging Colorado River, then up and around majestic buttes chiselled into inaccessible areas where Indian ruins are nestled in the Canyon walls. Apparently Navajo Indians had made this place their home for thousands of years in the distant past. When we got safely back to base from this 'flight of a lifetime' and having paid our fare of 125 dollars per person I thought, "Well that's it -I've seen all I'm going to see of the Grand Canyon." But it wasn't to be, our adventure had only just started!

A hundred metres away in a stoutly built wooden corral were ten or so dust covered mules in the process of being unsaddled. They had just returned from their daily jaunt to the Canyon floor. Now, a highlight of any South Rim visit is a ride down the trail on a mule. "Come on," I said to Ruth, "Lets find out more." I made enquiries from the guide, an Indian type with a deeply, sun-tanned leathery face. He was wearing a Mexican Stetson, a decorative coloured jacket and his legs were protected by leather chaps. Trying to look like riding mules was a habit of mine I said. "Have you any rides available?" "You're just lucky sir." He replied. "I've had a cancellation so I've got two mules free for tomorrow, usually people have to book a mule six months in advance. If you want to go down to the Colorado tomorrow, be here at 8.00 am sharp. Price is 60 dollars per person. That will include your guide and lunch. Just sandwiches and liquid refreshment. Nothing fancy of course. Wear some sensible clothing and some stout boots." he continued. "Great, we will be here." I heard myself say with undisguised audacity. I hadn't ridden for five years or more, Would I have the stamina and positive outlook to cope, I wondered. The prospect of eight hours in the saddle was rather daunting to say the least, and as for Ruth, I knew she was game enough to follow on any of my escapades.

So, come join me now on an armchair tour to places heard of by many, but seen by few. The magical realm called Grand Canyon Country.

I didn't sleep well that night, and I didn't fancy much breakfast. What had we got ourselves into this time? We were up and around early and 'on parade' at 7.30 am in good time to saddle up. Our mounts gave the impression of being very bored with the prospect of yet another tramp to the river and back. It had been difficult to know what clothes to wear. At that time of day it is quite chilly on the rim, but I knew we would have to shed attire as we dropped down into the depth of the canyon. By now our companions of the day were beginning to arrive, all very excited at the thought of the adventure to come. We soon realised that we were the only English present and certainly the oldest! We were asked by our guide our approximate weight who then allocated a mule suitable for our size. Ruth, by far the lightest amongst the buxom American ladies, was granted the smallest mule, but the guide loaded the poor, suffering beast with the days provisions for the whole group! The instructions for the day's ride were that our respective mules, would respond to their names, which in our case were Betty and Raven. We were to sit firmly and upright in the saddle and when a rest was called on the trail to turn our mounts towards the precipice. A rather frightful experience as I was to find out later, because Betty seemed to want to live dangerously by standing just a few inches from the edge of the drop!

Both Ruth and I had done some riding in our time, but to ride a mule was another first for both of us. However, once in the saddle I was amazed how big and strong these animals are, also, as we were to find out, very sure footed which was just as well, considering the narrow, twisting tracks that we had to negotiate. One behind the other with our guide leading, we were away dropping lower and lower into the depth, on some occasions the vertical cliff fell away for hundreds of feet, but I soon learnt to have faith in my mount. And as the boss man explained. "We try very hard to get our riders back to base in one piece, they don't pay until they are safely back on the rim."

The scenery is quite out of this world. A broad expanse of colourful minarets and buttes, a land of towering red and white cliffs and strange wind carved shapes one in particular like a Mexican Hat, another looked like a giant boat which was very imposing. And to recall that this great gap in the earth's surface has been carved out over millions of years by the elements. One has got to see it to believe it. Two hours later, already feeling stiff, we thankfully dismounted at a source of water and shade. The Indian Gardens, 3000 feet below the rim. We were more than thankful to rest in the shade for a while and demolish our provisions and I thought my mule was never going to stop drinking from the little spring. By now the heat from the sun was almost unbearable and there wasn't a breath of wind. One must appreciate that this canyon is eighteen miles from rim to rim at this point. The trail we were following is not downhill all the way, before us now was a flat, desert-like plain which we had to cross before starting another long descent to the river. A great opportunity to put our steeds into a canter. The mule at speed is a rather ungainly animal, more suited to heavy pack work. I wish this sight could have been captured on camera. Imagine our leader, yelling encouragement, Stetson hat held aloft as he lead his group of eight over-weight Americans and an English farmer and his long suffering wife. I gritted my teeth, clamped my knees into Betty's flank and held on for dear life.

Order of the mule skinners

When we did eventually stop the poor, suffering mules, hung their heads, gasped for breath and sweated profusely. I think our guide expected half his charges would have fallen off by now. We were all winded, yes, but still mounted. At last, after four hours mostly spent in the saddle, we dismounted and gazed down at the wild Colorado River. I couldn't believe that young adventurers white water raft these turbulent waters from end to end. We sat around for half-an-hour soaking up the unbelievable scenery before turning back, after all we faced another four hours or so in the saddle and I wasn't sure if Betty and Ruth's Raven would make it to the top.

It goes without saying that next morning we didn't rise early and when we did we felt muscles and joints we didn't know existed! However, it had been an experience I wouldn't have missed for the world.

We were to spend two more days around the area before heading back to LA. It is perhaps worth recording that before leaving the South Rim, Ruth purchased from the local Indians some beautiful pieces of jewellery made from silver and precious stones. A memento of Grand Canyon Country.

The long journey back to LA proved interesting. After driving a hundred miles or so through desert country, a road sign to the left read Little London 19 miles. I decided a visit worthwhile. I had remembered reading about the Americans purchasing a famous London Bridge and after it was dismantled, they shipped it across the Atlantic and subsequently erected it on dry ground in the desert, a much easier task than spanning a swift flowing river. Their next step was to divert the Colorado River and hey-presto they had a use for their bridge! Surely only Americans would attempt such a task? Little London is now completed with replicas of all the old houses, pubs and restaurants, even down to the red telephone boxes, the distinctive taxis and the double decker buses. We left 'London' rather late in the day with the intention of finding accommodation for the night at the next place of habitation. That turned out to be a mistake, we should have stayed where we were. Hotels, motels, even houses were few and far between in the Mojave Desert. It was not until we had driven nearly another hundred miles and with fuel getting desperately low that we hit a rundown community. At least it boasted a gas station and truckers stop-over. The only motel in the place was full and B&B's didn't exist, so we were forced to sleep overnight in our car parked amongst the gigantic lorries. We didn't get much sleep, at least I thought I hadn't. But Ruth disagreed. She said I had snored all night, ground my teeth and jumped around like I was still riding that darn mule back in the Canyon.

However we were up at dawn and into the cafe by 6.00 am, blurry eyed, unwashed and in my case unshaven. We certainly looked out of place and drew some curious glances. After studying the chalk written menu which hung on the wall, I placed our order with the man behind the counter. French fries, bacon and two eggs, sunny side up twice. He just nodded, half turned and shouted our requirements to someone working in the screened-off kitchen. By now he was already passing us two cups of black coffee. Making conversation he stated the obvious. "You two are new in town, just passing through I guess?" "That's right motel up the road was full so we slept in our car in your yard. Or tried to sleep, lorries kept pulling in all night that was the trouble, then somebody's dog decided to bark." I replied. "That'll be eighteen bucks, Sir, no charge for the bed." I passed him a twenty dollar bill, at the same time telling him to keep the change. I poured milk into our coffee before taking two seats at a vacant table in the corner. An hour later feeling refreshed after our early morning meal we took our leave. Checked our car for water and oil, bought some gas before leaving civilisation and were on our way once more. Eventually, after an uneventful drive, we reached the outskirts of LA and bravely faced the long drive back through the City. Once safely back at Mike and Gina's condominium we settled down for a few days rest before flying home to England.

Sometimes I ask myself. "Why did we go away in the first place?"

In conclusion.

Whenever I travel, either in this country or return from overseas, I am constantly struck afresh by the sheer beauty of the British countryside. It is one of the things which make this country of ours so special, particularly my Green Valley, in my eyes anyway. I would not wish to live anywhere else.

The End.